Ingredient Substitu

The beauty of cooking, is that you can make many substitutions without compromising the flavor profile. Below I've made a list of some ingredients that you could substitute if you are conscious of the lipid (fat/cholesterol) content or want alternatives.

- Ghee/butter Substitute with Olive Oil or Vegan Ghee
- Margarine can be substituted with Olive oil
- Vegetable/Sunflower oil Substitute with Olive/Avocado Oil
- Milk Substitute with lactose free Fat free milk or Rice milk
- Cream Substitute with Soy Milk and Olive Oil
- Sugar substitute with Agave nectar or Honey
- White basmati Substitute with brown basmati rice
- White bread Substitute with brown bread or other unsliced whole grain breads
- Beef/Chicken stock Substitute with Vegetable stock

Where to Find some ingredients

South African cuisines use a variety of ingredients, many of which you can find at local ethnic grocery stores or even online. I encourage you to use ALL ingredients in the recipes to get the flavor profile to be as close as possible to the authentic way food is prepared overseas. Freshly made is also preferred if possible. I grind some of my own spices.

- Curry leaves: Can be bought from small ethnic grocery stores or online on Amazon.
- Ground FRESH Ginger and ground Garlic: Most grocery stores have chopped versions and you can further grind it down or make your own or go to Asian grocery stores.
- Premade region-specific curry powders can be bought on Amazon or Etsy I prefer to make my own and have provided recipes for you too! Nothing beats Homemade Spices!
- Hominy(Maize/Samp) can be purchased at most grocery stores or local Mexican stores.
- Maize meal is called Polenta or Cornmeal or Pap/ugali in other regions and can be found in most grocery stores and even online. This is a finely ground version of Hominy/Maize.

What are Some of the Most Popular South African Spices?

Durban curry Powder

Durban curry powder comes from the city of Durban in the KwaZulu-Natal province(Where Shaka Zulu was born). It is considered one of the best curry powders in the world. Durban is the home of the majority of South Africa's 6th generation of Indian immigrants which is why many of the city's dishes have such a heavy Indian influence. Most of the descendants were from the states of Gujarat and Tamil Nadu, so the food from Durban tends to be on the spicy side.

Durban curry powder is red due to the use of cayenne pepper, Native to Mexico. The cayenne ensures that it is very hot, but sweet spices like cardamom and cinnamon are used in it as well. The result is a curry powder that is highly aromatic along with being spicy.

Cape Malay curry powder

Cape Malay curry powder has more of an influence from Malaysia and Java than from Southern India. It is milder and sweeter. The influence comes from Malaysian and Javanese slaves brought to South Africa by the Dutch.

Cape Malay curry powder places more of an emphasis on sweet spices like fennel seeds and cardamom done on hot ones like chilies. As a result, it is sweeter and not as hot as Durban curry. You can use it to make traditional Cape Malay dishes like bobotie and in the marinade for sosaties, the South African version of Middle eastern Shish kebab.

Braai salt(BBQ salt)

Braai which is a South African BBQ is one of the culinary traditions that all of South Africa's ethnicities have in common. Braai salt is a dry rub that can include ingredients such as mustard, coriander, and cumin. These spices may be used to cook meats ranging from beef and lamb to more game meat like ostrich/buck.

Fish Masala Seasoning

This homemade **Fish Masala** spice blend is perfect for your spicy fried masala fish, Cape Malay Pickled Fish,_and oven-baked masala fish or seafood recipes. This is a very commonly used seasoning in South African homes.

Peri-Peri Sauce

It is a spicy Chili pepper & garlic sauce, also known as Piri Piri or Pili Pili in Swahili, introduced in Angola and Mozambique when the Portuguese settlers came with African birds eye Chili Peppers or what they call, Piri Piri. The chicken/Seafood is marinated in Peri-Peri Sauce along with other seasonings before grilling them.

How to make a Durban Curry Powder?

Roasting spices releases the oils and adds a lot of flavor. To roast and grind seeds is simple: Place the seeds in a dry pan on a moderate heat until they become aromatic. Do not let the seeds burn, lift the pan and give it a shake to 'stir'. Give it a minute or two then simply grind in a spice grinder, pestle & mortar or even in a food blender.
The texture will be different with each method.

Ingredients
1 Tablespoon of ground Dhania powder (Corriander Powder)
1/2 Tablespoon ground Elaichi (Cardamom)
1/2 Tablespoon of Dalchini Powder (Cinnamon)
1/2 Tablespoon Methi (Fenugreek)
1 Tablespoon ground Jeera (Cumin)
1 Teaspoon ground cloves (teaspoon not tablespoon)
6 Tablespoons chili powder(Ground cayenne pepper)
1 Tablespoon Red Cayenne Pepper Powder (organic is best)
1/2 Adrak Powder (Ground Ginger Powder)

Directions

- Set out your ingredients separately
- Get a clean, dry, glass jar
- Roast your seeds, grind into a powder. Measure them out, as per the recipe, into the glass jar.
- Add your pre-powdered ingredients
- Close the lid and give a good shake to mix all the ingredients.
- Store in a cool, dry place and guard with your life!

You can also purchase ready made Durban curry powder online although the aroma is slightly compromised vs making it yourself.

How to make Garam Masala?

Garam masala translates to Hot spices although it's not spicy in heat. It is a blend of ground spices used extensively in Indian cuisine. The spices for garam masala are usually toasted to bring out more flavor and aroma, and then ground. Most of the Indian influenced curries in the recipes, will have this spice mix. You can make your own with the recipe below or purchase most of the ready mixed blends online on Amazon or many other stores.

Ingredients
1 tablespoon ground cumin
1 ½ teaspoons ground coriander
1 ½ teaspoons ground cardamom
1 ½ teaspoons ground black pepper
1 teaspoon ground cinnamon
½ teaspoon ground cloves
½ teaspoon ground nutmeg

Directions
Mix cumin, coriander, cardamom, pepper, cinnamon, cloves, and nutmeg in a bowl. Place mix in an airtight container, and store in a cool, dry place.

How to make Cape Malay Curry Powder?

Cape Malay curry is very distinctive and relies on bold fruity flavors and aromas (combining sweet and savory flavors) and are not quite as hot or spicy as some of the Indian curries. The Cape Malay curry is a special blend of spices not found in other dishes and originates from the "Bo-Kaap" area of the Cape.

Ingredients
1 tablespoon clove
½cup coriander seed
1 tablespoon fennel seed
1 tablespoon black mustard seeds
3 tablespoons fenugreek seeds
2 tablespoons black peppercorns
3 small dried hot red chilies, seeds and stems removed
3 tablespoons cumin seeds
¼cup ground cardamom
¼cup ground turmeric
1 tablespoon ground ginger
2 curry leaves, chopped into small pieces

Directions

Dry roast the whole seeds in a pan for a couple of minutes then grind them up in a food processor, grinder or with a pestle and mortar. Add the rest of the spices, chillies and curry leaves and store in an airtight container.

How to make Fish Masala Spice?

Fish Marsala is an iconic flavor profile found in homes that make seafood curries. This Homemade seasoning blend will uplift any Fish/Seafood dish bringing the authentic flavors of South Africa out.

Ingredients

15 ml coriander seeds --> I level tablespoon
5 ml fennel seeds--> I level teaspoon
5 ml cumin seeds --> I level teaspoon
5 ml black peppercorns --> I level teaspoon
4 cloves
15 ml red chili powder --> I level tablespoon
2.5 ml garlic powder--> 1/2 level teaspoon
2.5 ml powdered ginger --> 1/2 level teaspoon
2.5 ml cinnamon powder--> 1/2 level teaspoon
2.5 ml turmeric powder --> 1/2 level teaspoon

Directions

Dry roasting whole spices

Add the coriander, fennel, cumin, black peppercorns, and cloves to a small pan dry clean pan, and dry roast on medium heat until it smells fragrant.

Remove from the heat when you see the first wisps of smoke at about 2-3 minutes and continue to stir it off the heat in the pan to continue frying the spices.

Let the roasted whole spices cool before grinding.

Spice mix

If using a pestle and mortar, grind the spices until it is a fine powder, or as fine as you can. If using an electric spice grinder, pulse the spices until it is a fine powder. Try not to let the motor run for so long that the spices start to heat up, as it ruins the flavor.

Add the chili powder, garlic powder, ginger powder, cinnamon powder, and turmeric powder to a bowl and mix in the freshly ground spices.

Use immediately or store in a container with an airtight lid and store in the fridge until required.

How to make a Peri-Peri sauce?

Homemade Peri Peri sauce is simple enough to make. It requires no cooking, just some chopping, and processing of the ingredients. It's an oil-based sauce, ideal for dipping, grilling, or frying, and is GREAT with chicken and seafood.

Ingredients

I pound red chilies chopped – <u>African Bird's Eye</u> chilies, but you can substitute with Cayenne pepper, Thai Chili Pepper, Habenero peppers, or even Serrano peppers
4 cloves garlic chopped
I teaspoon smoked paprika
1/2 cup chopped cilantro
1/4 cup chopped basil
1/2 cup olive oil or vegetable oil
Juice from 1 lemon (lemon juice)
Salt to taste

Directions

Add all ingredients to a food processor or blender.
Process to form a smooth sauce to your preferred consistency. You can strain out some of the excess liquid if you'd like, or just use it as-is.
Store in a glass jar and refrigerate. This can be used to marinate chicken/seafood overnight ot add as a dipping sauce for bread when dipping

Kitchen Conversions

WEIGHT
1 GRAM = .035 OUNCES
100 GRAMS = 3.5 OUNCES
500 GRAMS = 1.1 POUNDS
1 KILOGRAM = 35 OUNCES

BASIC KITCHEN CONVERSIONS & EQUIVALENT
DRY MEASUREMENTS CONVERSION CHART
3 TEASPOONS = 1 TABLESPOON = 1/16 CUP
6 TEASPOONS = 2 TABLESPOONS = 1/8 CUP
12 TEASPOONS = 4 TABLESPOONS = ¼ CUP
24 TEASPOONS = 8 TABLESPOONS = ½ CUP
36 TEASPOONS = 12 TABLESPOONS = ¾ CUP
48 TEASPOONS = 16 TABLESPOONS = 1 CUP

LIQUID MEASUREMENTS CONVERSION CHART
8 FLUID OUNCES = 1 CUP = ½ PINT = ¼ QUART
16 FLUID OUNCES = 2 CUPS = 1 PINT = ½ QUART
32 FLUID OUNCES = 4 CUPS = 2 PINTS = 1 QUART = ¼ GALLON
128 FLUID OUNCES = 16 CUPS = 8 PINTS = 4 QUARTS = 1 GALLON

BUTTER
1 CUP BUTTER = 2 STICKS = 8 OUNCES = 230 GRAMS = 8 TABLESPOONS

METRIC TO US COOKING CONVERSIONS
OVEN TEMPERATURES
120 C = 250 F
160 C = 320 F
180 C = 350 F
205 C = 400 F
220 C = 425 F

BAKING IN GRAMS
1 CUP FLOUR = 140 GRAMS 1 CUP SUGAR = 150 GRAMS 1 CUP POWDERED SUGAR = 160 GRAMS 1 CUP HEAVY CREAM = 235 GRAMS

VOLUME
1 MILLILITER = 1/5 TEASPOON 5 ML = 1 TEASPOON 15 ML = 1 TABLESPOON 240 ML = 1 CUP OR 8 FLUID OUNCES 1 LITER = 34 FL. OUNCES

US TO METRIC COOKING CONVERSIONS
1/5 TSP = 1 ML
1 TSP = 5 ML
1 TBSP = 15 ML
1 FL OUNCE = 30 ML
1 CUP = 237 ML
1 PINT (2 CUPS) = 473 ML
1 QUART (4 CUPS) = .95 LITER
1 GALLON (16 CUPS) = 3.8 LITERS
1 OZ = 28 GRAMS
1 POUND = 454 GRAMS

WHAT DOES 1 CUP EQUAL ?
1 CUP = 8 FLUID OUNCES
1 CUP = 16 TABLESPOONS
1 CUP = 48 TEASPOONS
1 CUP = ½ PINT
1 CUP = ¼ QUART
1 CUP = 1/16 GALLON
1 CUP = 240 ML

BAKING PAN CONVERSIONS
9-INCH ROUND CAKE PAN = 12 CUPS
10-INCH TUBE PAN = 16 CUPS
10-INCH BUNDT PAN = 12 CUPS
9-INCH SPRINGFORM PAN = 10 CUPS
9 X 5 INCH LOAF PAN = 8 CUPS
9-INCH SQUARE PAN = 8 CUPS

BAKING PAN CONVERSIONS
1 CUP ALL-PURPOSE FLOUR = 4.5 OZ
1 CUP ROLLED OATS = 3 OZ
1 LARGE EGG = 1.7 OZ
1 CUP BUTTER = 8 OZ
1 CUP MILK = 8 OZ
1 CUP HEAVY CREAM = 8.4 OZ
1 CUP GRANULATED SUGAR = 7.1 OZ
1 CUP PACKED BROWN SUGAR = 7.75 OZ
1 CUP VEGETABLE OIL = 7.7 OZ
1 CUP UNSIFTED POWDERED SUGAR = 4.4 OZ

1-Umqhoshosho

A Xhosa Bean & Maize Dish:
(One of Nelson Mandela's Favorite Dishes)

NELSON MANDELA'S FAVORITE

PREPPING TIME: 20 MIN   **SERVES:** 2   **COOKING TIME:** 60MIN

Ingredients

- 3 1/3 cups dried red speckled beans, well rinsed &soaked overnight
- water to cover
- 1 small onion, chopped
- ½ cup leeks, chopped
- 2 cups Samp (Hominy/Maize), well rinsed
- 1 cube beef stock
- 3 tablespoons butter+ salt& pepper

Directions

1.Place the samp (Hominy/Maize) and beans together in a pot with water.

2.Cover and bring it to a boil and then reduce the heat and cook until soft for at least 2 hours. Do not stir or it will become excessively starchy.

3.Keep checking to ensure that the mixture does not stick at the bottom of the pot. Add water if necessary.

4.After about an hour, add the onion, leek and stock. Allow simmering until it is soft.

5.Add the butter and seasoning and stir with a wooden spoon. It must not be dry.

6.Serve with umleqwa or lamb curry.

- *Salt and pepper to taste.*

2-Isgwaqane

(Maize Meal & Red Speckled Beans)

PREPPING TIME: 20 MIN **SERVES:** 2 **COOKING TIME:** 1 HR 25MIN

Ingredients

- 3 pinch salt
- 1 pinch black pepper
- 4 cups water(946 ml)
- 2 cups of red speckled beans. Soaked Overnight.
- 3 cups Maize/Polenta/Corn meal
- 3 teaspoons of vegetable/olive oil

Directions

1. In a large saucepan place beans, a pinch of salt & 4 cups of water. Let it boil for 1 hour.
2. Once the beans start to get tender, add 3 cups of maize meal and stir using a wooden spoon until the maize meal and beans are nicely blended.
3. Leave for 30 minutes until the maize meal is fluffy and well cooked.
4. Add 3 teaspoons of oil and cook for another 10 minutes.

- *A perfect accompaniment to stews and potjies.*

3-Chakalaka & Pap (South African relish)

Ingredients

Chakalaka

- ¼ cabbage, sliced
- 1 onion, chopped
- 3 tomatoes, chopped
- 2 carrots, roughly grated
- 1 tbsp)Durban curry powder
- pinch cayenne pepper (optional)
- 2 cups canned red beans or baked beans
- salt and freshly ground black pepper, to taste

Pap

- 500ml (2 cups) water
- 2cups Maize meal/Corn meal
- salt, to taste
- 2 tablespoons butter

Directions

How to make chakalaka(Vegetable relish)

1. In a saucepan over medium heat, fry the onion, carrots, tomatoes and curry powder together, for 5 minutes.

2. Add the cabbage and season to taste, adding some cayenne pepper if you like it strong.

3..Stir in the beans, cover the saucepan and cook over low heat, for 30 minutes.

4.Taste at the end and adjust with a bit of sugar if it is too acidic.

Pap (Maize/Corn meal):

1.Boil the water in a saucepan, then add the maize meal and some salt.

2.Stir until combined, cover and cook over low heat, for 45 minutes, stirring every now and then.

3. *Stir in the 2 tablespoons of butter when the pap is ready.*

4-Shisha Nyama-Burn Meat
(BBQ)

A VARIETY OF MEAT GRILLED OVER COALS OR WOOD (NO GAS GRILLS)

Lamb chops, chicken drumsticks, wings, sausages, steaks and any meat you can think of.

Marinate the meats overnight for the best flavors:

Herbs to use for meat

- Chicken: Rosemary, basil, parsley, savory, French tarragon.
- Lamb: Rosemary, garlic, ginger, mint, lemon balm, thyme.
- Pork: Basil, coriander, chervil, marjoram, oregano, sage, thyme.
- Steak: Garlic, ginger, horseradish, mint, chives, parsley, thyme.

Ingredients to make a seasoning spice rub

- 2 tablespoons ground coriander
- 2 tablespoons smoked paprika
- 1 teaspoon garlic powder
- 1 teaspoon onion powder
- 1/2 teaspoon ground allspice
- 1 tablespoon dark brown sugar
- 2 teaspoons freshly ground black pepper
- 1/2 teaspoon ground cayenne1/2 teaspoon ground nutmeg

Mix all the ingredients together and marinate meats <u>overnight</u>

<u>Grill on a charcoal/wood fired grill for the authentic South African BBQ (Braai/Shisha Nyama)</u>

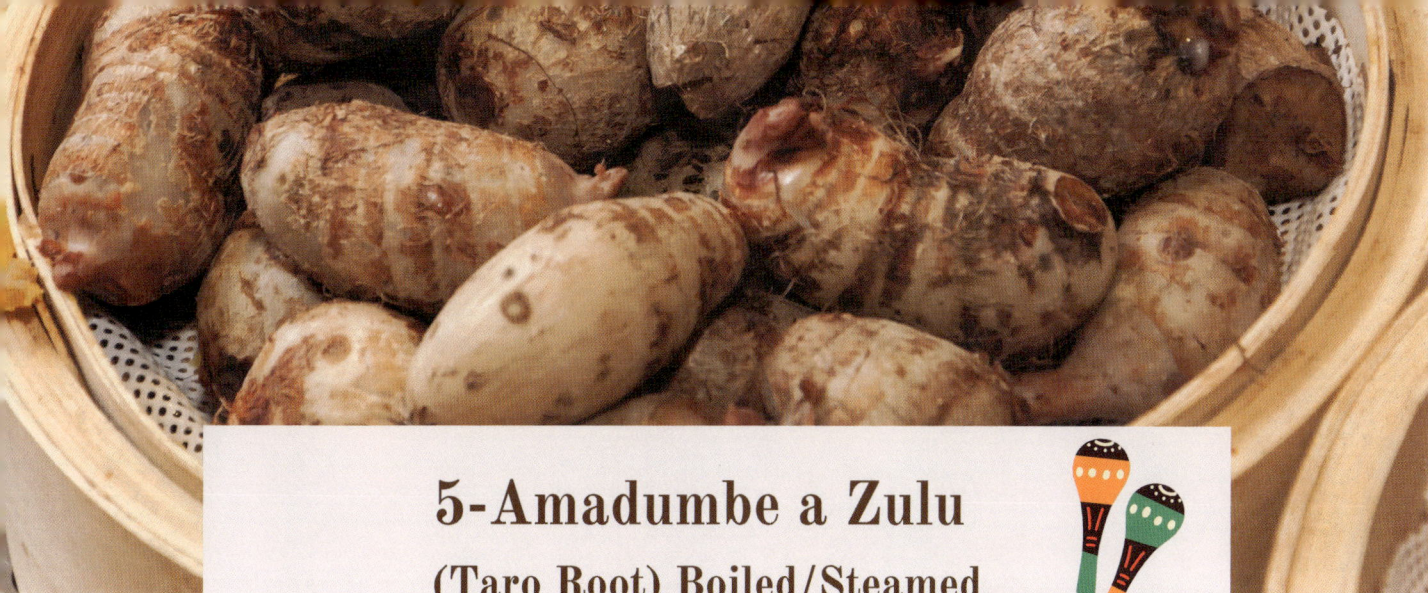

5-Amadumbe a Zulu
(Taro Root) Boiled/Steamed

PREPPING TIME: 15 MIN   SERVES:2   **COOKING TIME:** 30 MIN

Ingredients

- 5 Amadumbe/Taro Root
- 2 cups Water
- 1 teaspoon Salt to taste

Directions

1. Wash your amadumbe/Taro Root.

2. Put your amadumbe/Taro Root in a pot and add just enough water to cover half an amadumbe/Taro . Close pot with lid and bring to boil.

3. Turn down the heat and boil the amadumbe/Taro root for minutes or until you can stick a fork in your amadumbe/Taro root and it goes in easily. If water level drops during cooking add more water.

4. Remove pot from stove and drain any excess water.

5. Peel amadumbe /Taro and serve whole or cut in half.

Serve and enjoy!

6-Spinach Ujeqe
A Traditional Zulu Steamed Bread

PREPPING TIME: 20 MIN, 30 MIN STANDING TIME   **COOKING TIME:** 1 HOUR

Ingredients

- 2 cups flour
- salt, a pinch
- 1/4 Tsp Sugar
- 1/2 cup warm water
- 1 x 10 g sachet of dry yeast
- Metal bowl to fit inside a pot/saucepan
- 1/2 cup warm milk
- 1 large free-range egg
- 2 Tablespoon vegetable oil
- 3 cups baby spinach, chopped

Directions

1. Mix all the dry ingredients, then add the wet ingredients and spinach to form a dough.
2. You can knead the dough with your hands, but I prefer to use an electric mixer.
3. When all the ingredients are thoroughly combined, transfer the dough onto a dry surface and knead it into a small ball. The dough will be sticky.
4. Place the dough in a large, greased bowl and cover with cling wrap. Allow to stand in a warm place to rise for 30 minutes, or until it has tripled in volume.
5. Oil a medium-sized metal bowl.
6. Boil 4 cups water in a large saucepan. Knock down the dough and place it in the metal bowl over the saucepan.
7. Cover with the lid and cook over low heat for 1 hour, or until a knife comes out clean when inserted into the center of the bread.

- *Serve with any protein or veg dish of your choice.*

7-Slaai is a Swati Salad

PREPPING TIME: 20 MIN   **SERVES:** 2

Ingredients

- ½ teaspoon salt
- 3 tablespoons lemon juice
- 1 teaspoon fresh grated ginger
- ½ cup peanuts , crushed
- Radishes , thinly sliced (optional)
- 2 large avocados (ripe), diced into ½ inch/1cm cubes

Directions

1. Mix lemon juice, ginger and salt in a large bowl.
2. Add the avocado and mix gently.
3. Marinate at room temperature for 20 minutes.
- *Sprinkle with crushed peanuts, thinly sliced radishes (optional) and serve.*

8-Sidvidvu Pap-

Pumpkin Maize meal Porridge with Ostrich in Cream Sauce

PREPPING TIME: 25 MIN   **SERVES: 2**   **COOKING TIME: 45 MIN**

Ingredients for Pumpkin pap (maizemeal)

Prep Time 10 minutes & Cook Time 30 minute

- 2 +/- cups water
- 1/2 cup maize meal (pap/cornmeal)
- 1 small Pumpkin Peeled and cubed

Ingredients for Ostritch in cream sauce

Prep Time 15 minutes & Cook Time 20 minute

- salt to taste
- pepper to taste
- 3/4 cup red wine
- 1 cup white wine
- 1/2 cup heavy cream
- 5 Juniper berries lightly crushed
- 6 green peppercorns lightly crushed
- 1 medium onion peeled and sliced thinly
- 2 lbs. Ostrich Steaks cut into slices about 1/2" each
- 2 Tbsp butter divided for frying onions and ostrich

Directions

Instructions for Pumpkin pap (maize meal)

1. In a large pot combine the pumpkin and ground maize. Add in enough water to cover the pumpkin. Bring to a boil.

2. Boil for about 30 minutes and add more water if necessary. Cook until the pumpkin is tender.

3. Drain off any access liquid.

4. Mash the cooked pumpkin and ground maize together, and serve warm.

8-Sidvidvu Pap-
Pumpkin Maize meal Porridge with Ostrich in Cream Sauce

PREPPING TIME: 20 MIN   **SERVES:** 2   **COOKING TIME:** 30 MIN

Directions for Ostrich in cream sauce

1. In a bowl, combine the red wine, juniper berries, salt and pepper.

2. Add the sliced ostrich meat to the marinade and mix well.

3. Cover the bowl and **refrigerate overnight**

4. When you are near ready to eat, and your pumpkin pap is nearly ready, melt some butter in a skillet and saute the onions until brown.

5. Add in the peppercorns.

6. Stir in the white wine and heavy cream bringing to a gentle simmer.

7. Season the cream with salt and pepper to taste and set aside.

8. Discard the marinade from the bowl with the ostrich meat.

9. Heat butter in a frying pan and flash fry the marinated ostrich slices. This cooks quickly just a minute or two aside.

10. Serve the ostrich steaks on a platter and drizzle the cream sauce over the top.

- *Serve it with pumpkin pap for a wonderful African meal.*

9-Bobotie a Malaysian/Indonesian Influenced
Minced Meat & Egg Dish

PREPPING TIME: 25 MIN   **SERVES:** 2   **COOKING TIME:** 55 MIN

Ingredients

- 1 cup + 1/2 cup milk, divided
- 2 large onions, roughly chopped
- 1/2 teaspoon ground turmeric
- 2 garlic cloves, finely chopped
- 4 teaspoons medium curry powder
- Zest and juice of one medium lemon, divided
- 1 teaspoon dried herbs (whatever you've got around - oregano, basil, marjoram, etc.)

- 2 large eggs
- 4 bay leaves
- Salt and pepper
- 3 slices of bread
- 1/2 cup fruit chutney
- 4 teaspoons tomato paste
- 2 tablespoons olive oil
- 1 tablespoon apricot jam
- 1 1/2 pound ground beef
- 1 teaspoon ground cumin

Directions

> Bake this recipe in a cast iron skillet , it can go from stovetop to oven.

1. Preheat your oven to 350°F/176 C and Soak the bread in 1 cup of milk.

2. Heat the olive oil in a wide skillet set over medium heat. Once the oil is hot, add the onions, and cook until soft.

3. Add the curry powder, mixed herbs, ground cumin, turmeric, and garlic, and stirring constantly, allow to cook for a minute or two until the garlic is soft.

4. Add the ground beef, and cook, stirring frequently to break up any big chunks, until browned.

5. Once the beef is browned, remove the skillet from the heat, and stir in the chutney, apricot jam, all the lemon zest, half the lemon juice, tomato paste, and salt and pepper to taste. Mix well, give it a taste, and add more lemon juice, salt, and pepper as desired.

6. Squeeze the milk from the bread, reserving the milk for later, and soften and tear the bread into small pieces. Mix the bread into the beef mixture, and spread evenly into an oven-proof dish.

7. Strain the milk that has come from the bread, and add the remaining 1/2 cup of milk. Beat in the eggs, and season with 1/4 teaspoon salt and pepper to taste. Pour this over the meat, and decoratively scatter the bay leaves on top.

- *Bake, uncovered, at 350°F/ 176 C for 45 minutes, or until golden brown.*

10-Beef Tomato Bredie
Cooked in a Sweet Sour Sauce

PREPPING TIME: 30 MIN   **SERVES:** 2   **COOKING TIME:** 2 HOURS

Ingredients

- 2 tablespoons cake flour
- 1 tablespoon white vinegar
- 6 whole white peppercorns
- 1 tablespoon vegetable oil
- 1 dash Worcestershire sauce
- 1 cube beef bouillon cube
- 2 ¼ pounds fresh tomatoes, chopped
- ½ teaspoon freshly ground black pepper
- 3 ½ pounds lamb or mutton breast chops, chopped into portion

- 1 teaspoon brown sugar
- 2 bay leaves
- 1 teaspoon salt
- 1 large onion, chopped
- 2 medium potatoes, quartered (Optional)

Directions

1. Heat oil over medium-high heat in a large, heavy-bottomed saucepan. Dredge meat in flour, and cook in hot oil until well browned.

2. Stir in onions, and cook until onions are soft, about 5 minutes. Mix in tomatoes. Season with salt, black pepper, white peppercorns, bay leaves, brown sugar, vinegar, Worcestershire sauce, and beef bouillon cube. Cover, reduce heat and simmer for 1 hr 25min. Stir occasionally, making sure nothing sticks on the bottom of the pot.

3. Stir in the potatoes and cook for an additional 45 minutes, until the potatoes are done and the meat is tender.

11-Cape Malay Chicken Curry
With Yellow Rice

PREPPING TIME: 30 MIN   **SERVES:** 2   **COOKING TIME:** 1 HOUR 20 MIN

Ingredients

For the curry

- 2 tbsp mango chutney
- 5 cloves, 2 tsp turmeric
- 2 tbsp finely grated ginger
- 1 tsp ground white pepper
- 1 tsp coriander, 1 tsp cumin
- 400g can chopped tomatoes
- 2 3/4 cups potato , cut into chunks
- 1 large onion , finely chopped

For the yellow rice

- 50g butter
- 50g raisins
- 350g basmati rice
- 1 tsp golden caster sugar

- 2 tbsp sunflower or grapeseed oil
- 1 cinnamon stick , snapped in half
- 1 bunch of Cilantro, chopped
- 1 chicken stock cube, crumbled
- 4 large garlic cloves, finely grated
- 12 bone-in chicken thighs, skin removed
- seeds from 8 cardamom pods, lightly crushed
- 1 large red chilli , halved, deseeded and sliced

- 1 tsp turmeric powder
- ¼ tsp ground white pepper
- 1 cinnamon stick, snapped in half
- 8 cardamom pods , lightly crushed

Directions

1.Heat the oil in a large, wide pan. Add the onion and fry for 5 mins until softened, stirring every now and then. Stir in the garlic, ginger and cloves, and cook for 5 mins more, stirring frequently to stop it sticking. Add all the remaining spices and the fresh chilli, stir briefly, then tip in the tomatoes with 2 cans of water, plus the chutney and crumbled stock cube.

2.Add the chicken thighs, pushing them under the liquid, then cover the pan and leave to cook for 35 mins. Stir well, add the potatoes and cook uncovered for 15-20 mins more until they are tender. Stir in the coriander.

3.About 20 mins before you want to serve, make the rice. Put the butter, rice, raisins, sugar and spices in a large pan with 550ml water and 1/2 tsp salt. Bring to the boil and, when the butter has melted, stir, cover and cook for 10 mins. Turn off the heat and leave undisturbed for 5 mins.

Fluff up and serve with the curry.

12-Cape Malay Pickled Fish

PREPPING TIME: 30 MIN   **SERVES:** 2   **COOKING TIME:** 1 HOURS

Ingredients

- salt to taste
- ½ cup water
- 3 bay leaves
- 8 whole black peppercorns
- 4 whole allspice berries
- 2 teaspoons ground cumin
- 2 teaspoons ground coriander
- ½ cup vegetable/Olive oil for frying
- ½ cup packed brown sugar, or to taste
- 2 large onions, peeled and sliced into rings
- 3 pounds cod fillets, cut into 2 to 3 ounce portions
- 1 red chile pepper, seeded and sliced lengthwise
- 2 cups red wine vinegar
- 2 cloves garlic, chopped
- 2 cloves garlic, chopped
- 2 tablespoons curry powder
- 1 teaspoon ground turmeric
- 1 teaspoon fish masala

Directions

1. Heat the oil in a large skillet over medium-high heat. Season the fish with salt and place in the skillet. Fry on both sides until fish is browned and cooked through, about 5 minutes per side. Remove from the skillet and set aside

2. Fry the onions and garlic in the same skillet over medium heat until translucent. Add the peppercorns, allspice berries, bay leaves, and red chile pepper. Pour in the vinegar and water and bring to a boil. Stir in the brown sugar until dissolved. Season with curry powder, turmeric, cumin and coriander. Taste and adjust the sweetness if desired.

3. Layer pieces of fish and the pickling mixture in a serving dish. Pour the liquid over until the top layer is covered. Allow to cool then cover and refrigerate for at least 24 hours before serving.

13-Cape Malay Vegetable Curry

PREPPING TIME: 25MIN   **SERVES:** 2   **COOKING TIME:** 35 MIN

Ingredients

- 3 onions sliced
- 3-4 tablespoons veg/olive oil
- 4 carrots chopped
- 3 tablespoons vinegar
- 3/4 cup green beans
- 2-3 tsp cayenne chili powder
- 3-4 tablespoons tomato paste
- 2/3 of cauliflower cut into florets
- 1 1/2 tablespoons Cape Malay curry powder
- 1.2 cups frozen/fresh peas
- 1 tsp black mustard seeds
- 1 tsp tumeric powder

- 3 tomatoes chopped
- 3 garlic cloves sliced
- Salt and 3 green chilis (sliced)
- 2 tsp minced ginger
- 1 tablespoon ground coriander
- 3 tablespoon apricot preserves
- 4 curry leaves
- 1 tsp fennel seeds
- 1/2 cup soaked chickpeas (optional)

Directions

1. Heat oil in a medium frying pan and cook onions until they are very translucent, adding garlic, ginger, and green chilis, and mustard seeds, and fennel seeds. 8-10min

2. Add the Cape Malay curry powder, coriander, and chili powder, turmeric, and cook for another minute or two. Add curry leaves

3. Add the tomatoes and cook until paste forms.

4. Add the tomato paste, vinegar, apricot preserves, salt, and a little water.

5. Add chickpeas with 1 cup water and cook for 15min

6. Add green beans and cauliflower and more water(If needed), cover, and cook until tender for around 15-20min.

7. Add carrots and green peas to the curry and cook until the peas are cooked through and all the flavors meld for around 20-25min.

Serve with steamed Jasmin, basmati or a starch of your choice.

14

14-Cape Malay Shrimp Curry

PREPPING TIME: 25MIN   **SERVES:** 2   **COOKING TIME:** 30 MIN

Ingredients

- 1 tsp sugar + 1 tsp salt
- 2 teaspoons crushed garlic
- 1 tsp crushed dried chili pepper
- 1 green bell pepper, seeded and puréed
- 1 tsp turmeric + 2 tsp fish masala
- 1/4 cup sunflower oil (or other vegetable oil)
- 2 large onions, thinly sliced (at least 2 cups)
- 1 tsp ground cumin + 1 tsp lemon juice2 ripe tomatoes, skinned and puréed (could probably substitute canned)
- 2 pounds large, wild-caught shrimp (or 2 pounds of crayfish tails, in shells, or one large crayfish)

Directions

1. If using shrimp, remove shells and devein. Rinse and set aside. (If using the whole crayfish, wash well,
2. remove legs and tail, and set them aside. If using small crayfish, leave shells on).
3. Slice the onions and puree/grate tomatoes, pureeed green pepper, and garlic.
4. Fry the onions on medium heat until golden, about 5-10 minutes.
5. Add the tomatoes, green pepper, garlic, and dried crushed chili pepper and cook, stirring occasionally
6. for 10 minutes.
7. Make a paste from the cumin, fish masala, turmeric, lemon juice, sugar, and salt (add a little water if
8. necessary) and cook until the gravy thickens, about 10 minutes.
9. Add the shrimp (or crayfish) and cook over medium heat for 15 minutes.
- *Serve with basmati rice or naan.*

15-Sosaties

A chicken kebab seasoned with apricot sweet n tangy sauce

PREPPING TIME: 30MIN   **SERVES: 2**   **COOKING TIME: 30MIN**

Ingredients

The Meat:

- 3 ½ lbs chicken & 14 wooden skewers
- 4 onions & 1 yellow/orange/red pepper peeled and each onion cut crosswise into 2-3 pieces
- 2 zuchinnis sliced into chunks

The Marinade:

- 2 tsp salt + oil for panfrying
- ½ cup milk + ½ cup water
- 1 tbsp apricot jam
- 1 tbsp brown sugar
- ¾ cup white vinegar
- 1 tsp ground allspice
- 5 bay leaves bruised
- 1 tsp ground cinnamon
- 1 tbsp curry powder mild
- 2 onion cut into fine rings
- 2 tbsp coriander seeds crushed
- 4 cloves garlic crushed and chopped
- 1 tsp ground ginger or 1 tbsp grated fresh ginger heaped

Directions

1. Make the marinade first, as it has to cool down completely. Use a large pot.

2. Fry the onion rings in oil until light brown. Stir now and then.

3. While the onions fry, mix all the dry ingredients in a bowl.

4. Now, add al the liquid ingredients together in a bowl except for the milk and water. Add the jam, garlic, and fresh ginger (if you are using) to this mixture too.

5. When the onions are light brown, stir in the mixed dry ingredients, and fry for a minute or so to release the flavours. Add an extra splash of oil and stir.

15-Sosaties

A chicken kebab seasoned with apricot sweet n tangy sauce

PREPPING TIME: 25MIN   **SERVES:** 2   **COOKING TIME:** 30 MIN

6. Turn heat lower, and add the liquids and also add the bay leaves.

7. Stir well and simmer slowly until thickened. Now taste carefully: the sauce should neither be too acidic or too sweet but rather spicy and tangy. Adjust by adding either a little more vinegar or lemon juice, or more sugar.

8. Cool the sauce, and stir in the milk. It must be of a coating consistency. If you think it is too thick, add a little bit of water and stir well. Leave sauce in the pot, and cut up the meat.

9. Cut the meat into bite-sized chunks, not too small.

10. Arrange the chicken on the skewers, alternating the different ingredients. (You can add our variety too)

11. Take the pot of sauce, roll each sosatie skewer in the sauce, and pack in a plastic container. When all the skewers have been "sauced" up, poor the leftover sauce over the sosaties in the container. Seal airtight and marinate for a minimum of 30 minutes and up to 2 hours in the fridge.

12. Cook 10 minutes on each side in a pan/braai(BBQ) over medium-high heat tuning each side till the meat is cooked.

16-Bunny Chow

(A hollowed-out half or quarter loaf of bread filled with curry)-lamb Curry

PREPPING TIME: 40 MIN   **SERVES: 2**   **COOKING TIME: 50 MIN**

Ingredients

- 2 small cinnamon sticks & 5 curry leaves
- 1 tbsp. ground turmeric
- 37grams. garam masala
- Cilantro bunch and 2 grated carrots
- 3 medium tomatoes, chopped (2 cups)
- 1/4 cup plus 2 Tbsp. Sunflower or olive oil
- 2 large white onions, chopped (about 3 cups)
- 2 1/4 lb. boneless lamb shoulder or any protein, cut into 1-inch cubes
- 3 medium russet potatoes (1 3/4 lb.), peeled and cut into 1-inch cubes
- 2 teaspoons cayenne pepper
- 2 tablespoons heaped ground garlic paste
- 2 tablespoon ground heaped ginger paste

- 4 bay leaves
- 2 tbsp. kosher salt
- 1 unsliced loaf of bread (You can Purchase on etsy)
- 2 tablespoons Durban masala

Directions

1. In a large (8-quart) Dutch oven or heavy-bottomed pot, heat the oil over medium heat until it shimmers.

3. Add the onions, bay leaves, cinnamon sticks, turmeric, Durban masala, curry leaves and cayenne pepper and cook, stirring occasionally, until the onions are softened, about 5-8 minutes.

4. Stir in the garam masala and the garlic-ginger paste and cook for a few seconds, stirring to prevent the spices from burning. Do this on medium heat.

5. Add the tomatoes and bring to a simmer; let cook for 5 minutes.

16-Bunny Chow

(A hollowed-out half or quarter loaf of bread filled with a curry)-lamb Curry

PREPPING TIME: 40 MIN   **SERVES:** 2   **COOKING TIME:** 50 MIN

6. Add the lamb or any choice of protein and salt, stirring to coat the meat in the sauce and distribute the seasoning. Simmer, stirring occasionally, 15 minutes.

7. Stir in the potatoes and 2 cups water; bring to a boil, then reduce to a simmer. Cook, uncovered, until the meat is tender and potatoes are soft, about 40 minutes. Add a handful of cilanro leaves to the curry while it's cooking.

8. To serve, cut out most of the center of each bread quarter(you can order unsliced bread from Etsy or if your bakery offers that) and reserve it whole, making sure to leave some bread at the base of each loaf. Divide among 4 plates and fill the bread bowls with the curry mixture.

9. Place grated carrots at the top of the curry as a side salad accompaniment.

Garnish with the cilantro, and top or serve with the reserved bread pieces.

**Dip the bread in the gravy and eat it with your hands! Enjoy

17-Lamb Biryani
The South African, Indian way

PREPPING TIME: 60 MIN   **SERVES: 2**   **COOKING TIME: 1 HOUR 30 MIN**

Ingredients

Marinade

- 50 gram tomato paste
- 1/4 tsp ground cardamom
- 1/4 cup chopped mint
- 1 tbsp ground coriander
- 1 tbsp ginger/garlic paste
- 1 large onion fried until crisp
- 1 tsp ground fennel
- 6 curry leaves + 2 tsp garam masala
- 2 Roma tomatoes' skin removed and pureed
- 2 tsp ground cumin + Salt

- 1/4 cup chopped cilantro
- 1 tbsp kashmiri chilli powder
- 2 lb lamb pieces on the bone
- 1 tablespoon Durban masala + 1 tsp turmeric
- 1 tsp ground fennel/soomph
- 1 cup yogurt
- 3 whole green chillies

Dry spices should be slightly toasted on a dry frying pan to release oils & enhance flavor.

Rice

- 2 tsp Salt & 2 bay leaf
- 5 cloves & 2-star aniseed
- 6 large cloves peeled garlic
- 2-3 cups basmati rice
- 5 elachie/cardamom pods
- 2 cinnamon sticks & 2 black cardamom

Other Ingredients

- 100 gram butter
- 1/2 cup vegetable oil
- 1 tbsp vegetable oil
- 1 large onion fried until crisp
- 4 potatoes peeled and cut into wedges or cubes
- 1 cup green lentils cooked as per package instructions
- 1/3 cup yogurt for raita sauce to srve with cooked biryani

17-Lamb Biryani
The South African, Indian way

PREPPING TIME: 30 MIN   **SERVES:** 2   **COOKING TIME:** 1 HOUR 30 MIN

Directions

1. Slice the 2 onion, thin slices. Add half a cup of oil to a pan and fry the onion until golden and crisp. Drain on a paper towel

2. In a large glass bowl marinate the lamb with all the spices, herbs, tomato and tomato paste, and cup of yogurt and chillis. Mix in half the fried onion and reserve the other half for the biryani. Cover with a cling wrap and refrigerate overnight

3. When ready to cook the Biryani. Add the whole spices(toasted) as shown under "rice" to a pot with the rice. Season and cook as per package instructions. Rice shouldn't be fully cooked it should be parboiled., it will cook further in the oven

4. Once the rice is par boiled drain the water, depending on how you cook your rice. When ready to use the rice you will fluff it up with a fork. This will allow you to create different shades of yellow in the rice

5. In a large flat pot, heat 1 tablespoon oil and 2 tablespoon butter (from the 100gram butter). Mix in the marinated lamb and cook until it starts to dry up. Add a cup of water and cook further until lamb is tender.

6. Whilst the lamb is cooking you can steam your potatoes in the microwave for 5 minutes, season with salt and fry until slightly brown and crisp. If your potatoes cook quickly no need to steam them first

7. Once lamb is cooked mix in the lentils. Place the potatoes on top. Spread the rice over. Sprinkle the onion over and place the blobs of butter (the remaining 100g) all over the rice. Pour in a cup of water and cook in the oven at 180 degrees Celsius for 1 hour

8. Serve hot with raita which is a yogurt sauce(1 cup yogurt mixed with half chopped cucumber+finely chopped mint, 2 teaspoon garam masala, 1 teaspoon cumin) and a pinch of salt).

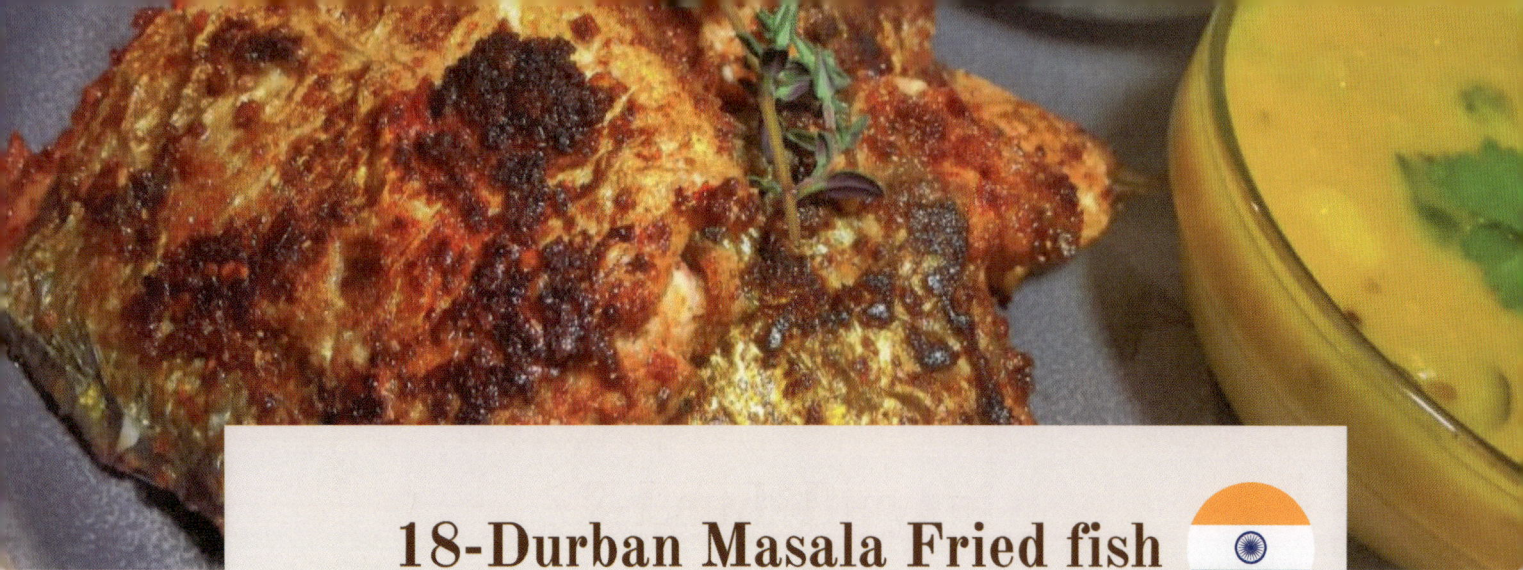

18-Durban Masala Fried fish

PREPPING TIME: 25 MIN   **SERVES: 2**   **COOKING TIME: 30 MIN**

Ingredients

- 300 grams Fish Fillets (either with or without skin on)
- 1 Tablespoon Ceyenne Chillie Powder
- 1/2 teaspoon Turmeric Powder
- 1/4 teaspoon salt or to taste
- 2 Tablespoon Lemon Juice
- 1/4 teaspoon White Pepper Powder
- 2 Tablespoon Olive Oil or Vegetable Oil
- 1 teaspoon Coriander and Cumin Powder
- 1/2 teaspoon Garlic Powder or 1 teaspoon fresh garlic paste/chopped

Directions

1. Make a paste with ingredients, and Rub onto fish fillets

2. Allow to marinate for 30 minutes

3. Heat 2 tablespoon olive oil in pan, When hot, place fish fillets, skin side down

4. Allow to cook for 3-4 minutes until skin begins to crisp

5. When skin is crispy, carefully flip over fish filets and allow to cook for a further 3 minutes or until done.

6. Add in 1 tablespoon butter or ghee to pan to help lift spices from pan.

7. Add in a few cocktail tomatoes and 1 or 2 sprigs of Fresh Dill and 1 tablespoon finely chopped fresh dill to pan. Allow to simmer until tomatoes are blistered.

- **Serve masala fish immediately** , preferably with skin side up, with a side of vegetables or salad

19-Durban Chicken Curry & Rice

PREPPING TIME: 20 MIN   **SERVES:** 2   **COOKING TIME:** 45 MIN

Ingredients

- 1 tsp vegetable oil
- 1 tsp ground cumin
- 1 tsp whole cumin
- 1 cup chicken stock
- 1 sprig of curry leaves
- Kosher salt, to taste
- 1 tsp ground coriander
- 1 inch fresh ginger, grated
- 1 teaspoon cayenne pepper
- 1 tablespoon tomato puree
- 4 cloves garlic, finely minced
- 1 to 2 whole cinnamon sticks
- 2 medium tomatoes, chopped
- 1 medium onion, finely chopped
- 2 tsp Durban curry powder,& 1 tsp garam masala powder
- 2 medium potatoes, diced into half-inch cubes
- 2 tsp ghee, or butter(you can substitute olive oil too)
- Fresh coriander leaves, for garnish, optional, 1 small rutabaga (swede), optional
- 8 pieces of chicken, preferably thighs and drumsticks or wings (2.2 pounds/1, kilogram)

Directions

1. Place the ingredients in a heavy-bottomed pan, melt butter with vegetable oil over low heat. Add curry powder, coriander, ground cumin, whole cumin, cayenne pepper, and cinnamon sticks and cook for about a minute or until fragrant. Be careful not to sear or burn the spices.

2. Turn heat to medium and add onion, ginger, and garlic and fry until softened. This should take about 3 minutes.

3. Turn heat to high and add chicken pieces. Allow meat to brown for about 5 minutes and coat pieces in onion and spices very well.

4. Add chopped tomatoes and tomato puree, and give the pot a good stir.

5. Throw in diced potatoes, rutabaga, chicken stock, and curry leaves. Let simmer for about 30 minutes on low to medium heat. Taste for seasoning and add salt if needed.

- *You can remove excess skin from the chicken. Chicken on the bone is tender and adds more flavor to the dish.*

19-Durban Indian Crab Curry

Ingredients

- 3-4 slit green chillies
- 1 sprig curry leaves
- 1 tsp cumin powder
- 2 tbsp ginger garlic paste
- 2 tbsp red chilli powder
- 1 tbsp coriander powder
- 1 tsp turmeric powder
- salt to taste & 1-2 cups water
- 1 can chopped or plum tomatoes
- 3-4 tbsp coconut oil or any other vegetable oil
- 6-8 small crabs, cleaned and cut into big pieces1 big onion chopped
- 1 tbsp tamarind paste or a lime sized tamarind soaked in warm water

Directions

1. Marinade the washed and cleaned crabs with 1 tbsp of ginger garlic paste, 1/2 tsp turmeric powder, 1 tbsp red chilli powder and keep aside for 5-10 minutes while you prep the rest of the ingredients.

24

19-Durban Indian Crab Curry

2. In a wide and thick bottom pan, add 2 tbsp of oil and heat up. Add the marinated crabs and fry until the crab shells change colour and turn slightly orange

3. take it out from the pan and set aside.

4. In the same pan, add the remaining oil and add the chopped onions and curry leaves. Fry until soft.

5. Next add remaining 1 tbsp of ginger garlic paste and saute until the onions are nicely browned.

6. Add all the remaining spice powders and saute for a minute.

7. Next add the can of chopped or plum tomatoes along with salt and stir to ensure everything is mixed

8. Cover and cook for 5 minutes on a medium flame until you see the oil floating at the top

9. Now add the tamarind water or paste and let the mix come to a simmer

10. Gently tip in the previously fried crabs and add 1-2 cups of water to adjust gravy

11. Mix everything until all the masala coats the crabs and simmer covered for 10-15 minutes until the crabs are cooked and the oil floats on top. Tip in the slit green chillis into the gravy just before you turn off the flame.

12. Let the curry rest for at least 10-15 minutes before you serve to let the flavours develop.

Serve with basmati rice or naan bread.

20- Pumpkin Curry

PREPPING TIME: 25MIN   **SERVES: 2**   **COOKING TIME:30 MIN**

Ingredients

- 1 Pumpkin (500g) - Butternut or Squash
- 25 ml Cooking Oil
- 1 tsp Mustard Seeds
- 1 tsp Salt
- 1 tsp Cummin Seeds
- 4 tsp Sugar
- 1 Chopped Onion
- 6 Dried Chilies or Green Chilies
- Curry leaves and few cilantro leaves

Directions

1.Skin the Pumpkin, Squash or Butternut.

2.Remove seeds and cut into cubes.

3. Wash and drain.

4. 2Heat oil; add Onion, Dry Chilies, Mustard Seed and Cumin Seeds.

5.Fry until golden brown, add Pumpkin and Salt, Sprinkle sugar and stir.

6. Cook on low heat until soft.

- *Stir and sprinkle with cilantro*
- *Serve with roti bread or basmati rice*

21-Soy Sausage Chutney

PREPPING TIME: 25MIN   **SERVES:** 2   **COOKING TIME:** 30MIN

Ingredients

- Oil, for frying
- Salt, to taste
- Half ground garlic
- One onion, chopped
- One teaspoon of sugar
- Spring onions, to serve
- Two sliced green chillies
- Four to five curry leaves
- Chopped Cilantro to taste
- Four to five chopped tomatoes
- Half a teaspoon of chili powder
- One box of Soy Sausages
- Half a teaspoon of ground ginger

Directions

1. Heat a bit of oil in a frying pan. Once hot, onions. Cook until onions are glassy or transparent colour and add a pinch of salt.

2. Move the frying pan away from the heat and add garlic, ginger, chilli powder, and curry leaves and add a little bit of water to prevent burning.

3. Place the frying pan over the heat again and stir slowly. Add in tomatoes and sugar and stir together. Then add in green chillies and stir once more.

4. Allow the tomatoes to break up and add water if necessary to prevent burning. Place lid over the frying pan and allow to simmer for four to five minutes.

5. Ensure that the tomatoes cook down nicely and that there is a saucy mixture.

6. Add in Fresh Cilantro and Soy Sausages.

7. Coat the Soy Sausages in the tomato chutney. Cover the lid and simmer for three to five minutes.

- *Finish it off by garnishing with spring onion.*

27

22-Durban TinFish

(Pilchard/Sardines in a can) Chutney

PREPPING TIME: 15 MIN　　　**SERVES: 2**　　　**COOKING TIME: 25 MIN**

Ingredients

- 2 boiled eggs
- 2 tablespoons veg/olive oil
- 1 level tablespoon Cayenne chili powder
- 2 teaspoon Durban masala
- 1 medium-sized onion finely chopped
- 1 cup fresh cilantro and green onions
- Quarter teaspoon ginger and garlic paste
- 3 or 4 green chilies (adjust to your liking)
- 1 large can of tin fish (pilchards in tomato sauce)
- Salt to your preferences although canned fish may already had salt

Directions

1. Heat a heavy pan on medium heat. Add oil
2. Fry the onions and green chilies until slightly soft
3. Add the chili powder for 2-3 minutes
4. Clean the tin fish by removing the bones. Add fish to the pan and mix gently into the mixture.
5. Remove from heat.

- *Serve warm or cold with roti/naan or bread.*

23-Lamb Chops Chutney Durban Style 🇮🇳

PREPPING TIME: 25 MIN   SERVES: 2-3   **COOKING TIME:** 30MIN

Ingredients

Ingredients for marinating:

- 1 tbsp of oil
- 8 lamb loin chops
- salt & pepper to taste
- dried parsley flakes (optional)
- 2 teaspoons Durban masala

To make the Durban chutney recipe:

- 1 tsp sugar
- 1 tbsp of oil
- 1 onion diced
- 1/2 tsp cumin seeds
- 1 tsp garam masala
- 1 tsp salt & pepper
- 1 fresh red chili sliced
- 1/2 tsp turmeric powder
- 6 cloves of minced garlic
- 1/4 tsp chili powder (adjust to taste)
- large tomatoes diced or grated (you can use either fresh tomatoes or canned ones, but i always try use fresh)

23-Lamb Chops Chutney Durban Style 🇮🇳

PREPPING TIME: 30MIN   **SERVES: 2-3**   **COOKING TIME: 35MIN**

Directions

1. Rinse the lamb chops under cold running water and pat them dry with a paper towel until they are completely dry. Sprinkle the chops with salt and pepper and dried parsley and Durban masala.

2. Heat up your oil on medium heat and once it's nice and hot, put your chops on the pan. Fry them for 3-5 minutes on each side until they are golden brown.

3. Once done frying, take them off the pan and place them on a side plate to rest. Do not wash the pan!

4. On the same pan, add 1 tbsp of oil and cook the diced onion on medium heat for 5 minutes.

5. Add the minced garlic and sliced chilly and cook for additional 2 minutes.

6. While it's frying, in a separate small bowl, mix up your chilly powder, turmeric, jeera seeds, garam masala, salt, sugar, and pepper. Add the spice mix to the onion-garlic-chilly mix and fry for an additional 2 minutes on low heat to open up the spices.

7. Add the diced tomatoes and about 1/2 cup of water to the pan and cook on medium heat for 10 minutes.

8. Once the tomatoes are done cooking, add the lamb loin chops back onto the pan and coat them with all the delicious tomato mix.

- *Garnish with fresh cilantro leaves if you desire.*
- *Serve with rice, roti or mashed potatoes.*

24-Tuna fish cakes

PREPPING TIME: 25 MIN **SERVES: 2** **COOKING TIME: 25 MIN**

Ingredients

- 1 Egg Whisked
- Olive Oil To Fry
- 1 Tbsp Mayonnaise
- 2 Cans Tuna Drained
- 1 Spring Onion Sliced
- Pinch Parsley Chopped
- Salt & Pepper To Taste
- 1 Tbsp Chutney(store bought)
- 3 Slices Bread Crumbed (Using Food Processor)

Directions

1. Put the bread in a food processor and pulse until it crumbs.
2. Mix together the whisked egg, mayo, chutney and seasoning (salt and pepper).
3. Add the chopped parsley.
4. Add the tuna to the egg and mix well.
5. Stir in the spring onions and breadcrumbs and combine.
6. Shape the tuna mixture into medium sized fishcakes.
7. Heat a little oil in a heavy-based frying pan. Fry the fishcakes over a moderate heat for +- 3 minutes on each side or until cooked and golden brown.

25-Lamb, Chicken, or Veg Potjie

(Dutch-style Caldron Pot Stew made over a Fire)

PREPPING TIME: 30 MIN   **SERVES:** 2-3   **COOKING TIME:** 2 HOURS

Ingredients

- 5 bay leaves
- 1 bottle red wine
- 2 mutton stock cubes
- 5 cloves garlic, whole or roughly chopped
- 4.4 lbs lamb, cut up in big chunks (you can use beef, chicken or even a mixture of your own veg here)

- 2 onions, roughly chopped
- Olive oil or butter for browning
- 5 sprigs of rosemary and thyme
- Assorted vegetable chunks. You can use pumpkin, potatoes, carrot, baby marrow and whatever else you might like.

Directions

1. Start off by dissolving the stock cubes in about 8cups of water and set aside.

2. While your potjie is heating up and the coals are getting ready, toss the lamb in some flour, salt and pepper. Add the olive oil or butter – depending on what you're using – to the pot and get some color on your lamb.

3. Once browned, add the stock, wine, garlic, herbs and onions to your potjie along with the lamb.

4. Let the potjie stew on a low heat for at least an hour and a half. **The key is NOT TO TOUCH IT.** Don't stir, don't prod, no matter how tempted you are. If you see the liquid has reduced too much, add a bit more.

5. After about an hour and a half, gently prod the lamb to see if it's soft. If it is, add all your veggies, cover and cook until the veggies are soft about another 30 minutes.

Serve with white rice or bread.

26-Vetkoek
(South African Traditional Fried Bread)

PREPPING TIME: 30 MIN   **SERVES:** 2   **COOKING TIME:** 20MIN

Ingredients

- 2 teaspoons salt
- ¼ cup white sugar
- 3 cups oil for frying
- 7 cups all-purpose flour
- 2 cups lukewarm water
- 1 (.25 ounce) package active dry yeast

Directions

1. Mix lukewarm water, sugar, and yeast in a small bowl. Let stand until yeast softens and begins to bubble slightly, about 5 minutes.

2. Sift flour and salt together in a large bowl.
3. Pour water mixture over flour mixture and knead until dough is smooth and elastic, 5 to 7 minutes. Cover bowl with clean cloth and let dough rise until unti doubled in volume, about 45 minutes.
4. Pinch off a piece of dough about the size of a tennis ball; roll until smooth. Flatten ball of dough until it is the size of palm; set aside on a floured work surface. Repeat with remaining dough.
5. Heat oil in a deep-fryer or large saucepan to 350 degrees F (175 degrees C).
6.Fry flattened pieces of dough in the hot oil, 2 to 3 pieces at a time, until golden brown, about 3 minutes per side

27-Afrikaans Frikedelle (meatballs)
with Sheba (Sweet Herby Tomato) Sauce

PREPPING TIME: 25MIN   **SERVES:** 2   **COOKING TIME:** 25 MIN

Ingredients

- 1 egg
- 1 tsp salt
- ½ tsp turmeric
- 2 Tbsp parsley
- 1 onion, minced
- pinch ground cloves
- 1 tsp unsalted butter

- 2 garlic cloves, minced
- ½ tsp ground black pepper
- 1 lb ground beef (85% lean)
- 1 tsp ground coriander seeds
- 2 slices white bread, soaked in water and squeezed dry

Directions

1. Tear the slices of bread and place them in a bowl. Cover the bread with water and set aside to soak.

2. In a medium skillet, heat the butter. Add the onion and garlic and sauté over medium high heat until golden, 5-6 min. Remove the onion mixture from the pan and set aside.

3. In a large bowl, combine ground beef with the seasonings and onion mixture. Squeeze the soaked bread as dry as you can get it and add it to the beef mixture along with the egg. Mix well, using your hands. Shape the meat mixture into balls, using roughly 2 Tbsp of meat for each. Place the shaped meat onto a plate and flatten the balls slightly.

4. Heat the skillet over medium heat and fry the meat patties 5-6 minutes on the first side and 3-5 minutes on the second side, until golden and firm.

5. Remove the patties from the skillet onto a clean, paper towel lined platter. Continue until all the frikkadel have been cooked.

Serve the frikkadel with mashed potatoes and sheba sauce (see recipe below).

Sheba Sauce

PREPPING TIME: 10 MIN   **SERVES:** 2   **COOKING TIME:** 25 MIN

Ingredients

- ½ tsp salt
- ¼ tsp sugar
- 2 onions, diced
- 1 Tbsp unsalted butter
- 2 garlic cloves, minced
- 1 Tbsp fresh oregano, chopped, or 1 tsp dry
- 1 Tbsp fresh parsley, chopped, or 1 tsp dry
- 4 tomatoes, diced (or 2-14.5 oz cans, slightly drained)

Directions

1. Heat the butter in a large skillet. Add the onions and garlic. Sauté over medium high heat until the onions have softened, 10 minutes.

2. Add the remaining ingredients, stir and bring the mixture to a simmer.

3. Cook, uncovered, for 15-25 minutes until the sauce has thickened slightly.

4. Sheba sauce makes a great accompaniment to mashed or boiled potatoes, rice, chicken, or any protein.

28-Pampoen Koekies
(Pumpkin fritters)

PREPPING TIME: 30 MIN   **SERVES: 2**   **COOKING TIME: 35** MIN

Ingredients

- 2 cups cooked pumpkin, mashed
- 1egg, beaten + 1 ml salt
- 33 grams or 1/8 cup flour
- 2 teaspoons baking powder
- margarine or Veg oil

Garnish

Sugar, mixed with:

- cinnamon
- lemon slice

Directions

1. Combine the pumpkin, flour, baking powder and salt to form a soft batter.
2. Add the egg and beat well.
3. Heat the butter, margarine or oil in a frying pan until it sizzles.
4. Drop spoonfuls of the batter in the oil and fry the fritters on both sides until slightly browned.
5. Remove and keep warm.

- *Serve hot, sprinkled with sugar and cinnamon and garnished with slices of lemon.*

29-Booreboontjies
(Mashed Green Runner Beans)

PREPPING TIME: **30** MIN   SERVES: 2   COOKING TIME: **30**MIN

Ingredients

This simple vegetable dish is made with only three main ingredients:

- 2 cups green runner beans
- 2 medium potatoes
- 1 large onion
- *You will also need a lump of butter and salt and pepper.*

Directions

1. To make mashed green beans, simply chop the beans and onions into 1 cm pieces, and quarter the potatoes.

2. Place the beans and onions in a pan of cold salted water. Bring to the boil, cover with a lid and then let them continue to boil for 5 minutes. Add the potatoes and continue boiling until the potatoes are soft enough to mash.

3. Drain in a Strainer, then add the butter, and plenty of ground black pepper and mash with a potato masher until well combined.

(keep texture chunky)

30-Mieliebrood
(Sweetcorn Bread)

PREPPING TIME: 30 MIN   **SERVES:2**   **COOKING TIME: 45 MIN**

Ingredients

- 1 leveled teaspoon salt
- 1/2 teaspoon paprika
- 2 eggs, beaten
- 60 ml/2 oz warm milk
- 350 g or 1 3/4 cups self-raising flour
- 410 g or 1 & 1/2 cups creamed sweet corn
- 60 g or 1/4 cups Baking Margarine, melted (measured into 2 bowls of 30g each)

Directions

1. Place sweet corn, eggs, salt, milk, and 30g of Baking Margarine into a bowl and stir.

2. Mix in flour and paprika to form a dough.

3. Brush a bread tin with melted Baking Margarine, dust with flour, and pour in the dough.

4. Bake at 170°C /330F for about 45 minutes or until well risen and lightly browned.

5. Brush with the rest of the melted Baking Margarine to keep the top soft.

31-Sheperds Pie

PREPPING TIME: **30** MIN   SERVES: **2-3**   COOKING TIME: 50 MIN

Ingredients

Meat Filling:

- 1 cup beef broth
- 1/2 teaspoon salt
- 2 tablespoons olive oil
- 2 garlic cloves -minced
- 1/2 cup frozen corn kernels
- 2 tablespoons tomato paste
- 2 tablespoons all-purpose flour
- 2 teaspoons dried parsley leaves
- 1 teaspoon dried rosemary leaves
- 1/2 teaspoon ground black pepper
- 1 tablespoon Worcestershire sauce
- 1 cup chopped yellow onion1 teaspoon dried thyme leaves
- 1 cup frozen mixed peas & carrots*
- 1 lb. 90% lean ground beef -or ground lamb

Potato Topping:

- 1/4 teaspoon ground black pepper
- 8 tablespoons unsalted butter -1 stick
- 1/2 teaspoon salt & 1/3 cup half & half
- 1/4 cup parmesan cheese & 1/2 teaspoon garlic powder
- 11/2 - 2 lb. russet potatoes -about 2 large potatoes peeled and cut into 1 inch cubes

31-Sheperds Pie

PREPPING TIME: 30 MIN   SERVES: 2-3   COOKING TIME: 50 MIN

Directions

Make the Meat Filling:

1. Add the oil to a large skillet and place it over medium-high heat for 2 minutes. Add the onions. Cook 5 minutes, stirring occasionally.

2. Add the ground beef (or ground lamb) to the skillet and break it apart with a wooden spoon. Add the parsley, rosemary, thyme, salt, and and pepper. Stir well. Cook for 6-8 minutes, until the meat is browned, stirring occasionally.

3. Add the Worcestershire sauce and garlic. Stir to combine. Cook for 1 minute.

4. Add the flour and tomato paste. Stir until well incorporated and no clumps of tomato paste remain.

5. Add the broth, frozen peas and carrots, and frozen corn. Bring the liquid to a boil then reduce to simmer. Simmer for 5 minutes, stirring occasionally.

6. Set the meat mixture aside. Preheat oven to 400 degrees F.

Make the potato topping:

1. Place the potatoes in a large pot. Cover the potatoes with water. Bring the water to a boil. Reduce to a simmer. Cook until potatoes are fork tender, 10-15 minutes.

2. Drain the potatoes in a strainer. Return the potatoes to the hot pot. Let the potatoes rest in the hot pot for 1 minute to evaporate any remaining liquid.

3. Add butter, half & half, garlic powder, salt, and pepper. Mash the potatoes and stir until all the ingredients are mixed together. 4. Add the parmesan cheese to the potatoes. Stir until well combined.

Assemble the casserole:

1. Pour the meat mixture into a 9x9 inch baking dish. Spread it out into an even layer. Spoon the mashed potatoes on top of the meat. Carefully spread into an even layer.

2. If the baking dish looks very full, place it on a rimmed baking sheet so that the filling doesn't bubble over into your oven. Bake uncovered for 25-30 minutes.

** *Cool for 15 minutes before serving.*

40

32-Fish & Chips

PREPPING TIME: 30 MIN	SERVES: 2	COOKING TIME: 15 MIN

Ingredients

For the Chips:

- 2 L sunflower Oil for frying and salt for sprinkling
- quality British Malt Vinegar, for serving
- 4 large Russet potatoes or other high starch/low moisture potatoes, peeled, sliced thickly, and put in a large bowl of cold water until ready to fry

Directions

For the Chips:

warm oven up.

1. Heat the oil in a deep fryer or a large heavy pan or Dutch oven until the temperature reaches over high heat until it reaches 325 degrees F (I use a cooking thermometer).

2. Thoroughly drain the sliced potatoes and blot them with paper towels to remove excess water. Once the oil is 325 F carefully fry the potatoes in small batches to avoid overcrowding and fry for 2-3 minutes until pale and softened. Use a slotted spoon to remove them from the oil and let them cool to room temperature.

3. Increase the temperature to 375 degrees F. Carefully add the fries again, frying in small batches, until they are golden brown and crispy, another 2-3 minutes. Remove with a slotted spoon, place them on a baking sheet or roasting rack, sprinkle with salt while they're still very hot, and place them in the warmed oven while you're frying the fish.

32-Fish & Chips

PREPPING TIME: 30 MIN   **SERVES:** 2   **COOKING TIME:** 15 MIN

Ingredients

For the Fish:

- 1 cup all-purpose flour & 1 teaspoon baking powder
- 1 teaspoon salt extra flour for dredging , chilled
- 1 1/4 cups light beer , VERY COLD
- 1 1/2 pounds fresh cod, haddock or halibut , (or other firm-fleshed white fish), cut into 4 pieces and patted dry (important for enabling the batter to adhere) oil for frying
- use beef tallow instead of oil for the best traditional flavor (follow linked tutorial which is the same method for beef fat as it is for pork fat).

Directions

For the Fish:

1. Combine the flour, baking powder and salt in a large flat bowl. Pour in the cold beer and whisk until smooth (use the batter immediately, do not let it rest for a while). In another large flat bowl add some extra flour for dredging.

2. Blot the fish with paper towels to remove excess moisture. Thoroughly dredge all sides of the fish in the flour and shake off the excess.

3. Dip the fish into the beer batter to thoroughly coat all sides, allowing some of the excess batter to drip off (but not too much!).

4. For Frying the Fish: You can either use a deep fryer or you can use a medium-sized skillet and fill it with oil to a depth of about an inch.

5. Heat the oil to between 350 F and 375 F, using a candy thermometer. Carefully drop the fish into the oil.

6. Fry the fish in the deep fryer for 5-8 minutes or until nicely golden. If using a frying pan fry the fish for about 2 minutes on each side or until nicely golden. Remove the fish with a slotted spoon, letting the oil drop off, then place the fried fish on paper towels for a few seconds and serve immediately. (If you wait too long to serve the batter will lose its crispiness.)

7. Serve with the chips, a sprinkling of quality British malt vinegar .

33-Sunday Beef Roast

Ingredients

- Olive oil
- English mustard
- Prepared horseradish
- 2 tablespoons runny honey
- 2 1/2 pounds russet potatoes
- One (5-pound) rib roast of beef bone-in
- 1/2 bunch fresh rosemary (about 5 sprigs)
- 1 heaping teaspoon sea salt plus more to taste
- 1 heaping teaspoon white or black peppercorns
- 1 pound of turnips (or substitute carrots)
- 6 tablespoons red wine vinegar or cider vinegar
- 1 whole head of garlic separated into cloves but not peeled
- 10 bay leaves (yes, 10—although they could be optional/adjusted)
- 3 1/2 tablespoons (1 1/2 oz) unsalted butter at room temperature

Directions

1. Take the beef out of the fridge about 30 minutes before you intend to cook it.

2. Preheat the oven to 475°F (246°C) and put your largest, sturdiest roasting pan in it to heat.

3. Bash the leaves from 2 sprigs rosemary into a paste with a heaping teaspoon each of salt and peppercorns. Add a drizzle of olive oil and rub this paste all over the beef. Place the beef straight in the hot roasting pan, fatty side up, and roast it, uncovered, for 50 minutes if you want your roast rare to medium-rare, a little longer for medium. The temperature of the roast will continue to rise after you take it out of the oven and let it rest.

4. Meanwhile, put a large pan of salted water on to boil. Peel the potatoes and turnips, then halve or quarter them and cut them into roughly 1-inch chunks. Add them to the boiling water, return to a boil, and then cook until somewhat tender, about 10 minutes. Drain the root vegetables in a colander and toss them a few

33-Sunday Beef Roast

PREPPING TIME: 30 MIN   SERVES: 2-3   COOKING TIME: 1 HOUR 30 MIN

times to expel any excess moisture, and then let them dry. (They can sit here for as long as needed.)

5. Carefully transfer the roast to a plate and set the roasting pan aside. Leave the oven on. Dot half the butter (let's just say 2 tablespoons although there's no need to be that precise) on top of the meat, then use the remaining rosemary sprigs to brush the honey all over the meat. Cover with a double layer of aluminum and a kitchen towel and let it rest for 30 minutes. Set the rosemary sprigs aside but don't discard them.

6. While the meat rests, quickly press/smash the unpeeled cloves of garlic, then add them to the fat in the hot roasting pan along with the rest of the butter and the 15 bay leaves. Pour in the vinegar and place the pan over 1 or 2 burners turned to medium-high heat. Add the potatoes and turnips. Keep moving everything around and season well with salt and pepper. When everything is sizzling away, put the roasting pan with the vegetables back into the hot oven for 30 minutes, or until crisp and golden.

7. When the vegetables are very nearly done, carve the beef. (If the meat was tied by your butcher, discard any string. Pour any juices that collected on the plate into a small heatproof dish and place it in the oven to keep warm. Grab a carving knife and first detach the roast from the bones in a single swoop by sliding the knife between the rib bones and the roast. Trim the upper cap, or fatty fat fat portion, of the roast and then trim and discard the visibly fatty portion of the cap (see bottom right portion of the photo) and thinly slice the remaining meaty section (see upper left portion of the photo). Slice the roast into chops by slicing between where the rib bones were (see center of the photo). Chop the meaty ends of the ribs (see upper right portion of the photo) from the rib bones (see bottom right).

8. Use the rosemary sprig brushes from earlier to paint the various cuts of meat with the flavorful juices left on the cutting board. Serve the meat with the hot, crisp vegetables, the dish of hot juices, and a good schmear of horseradish and mustard.

34-Irish Lamb Stew

PREPPING TIME: 20 MIN   **SERVES:** 2-3   **COOKING TIME:** 2 HOURS

Ingredients

- 1 bay leaf
- 2 teaspoons sugar
- 1/2 cup dry white wine
- 1 teaspoon dried thyme
- 1/2 cup all-purpose flour
- Chopped parsley, garnish
- 1 large yellow onion, finely chopped
- 4 cups chopped carrots (1-inch pieces) or Zucchini
- 4 cups store-bought or homemade beef stock
- 6 pounds boneless lamb shoulder, cut into 2-inch pieces
- 1/2 teaspoon freshly ground black pepper, plus more to taste
- 3 pounds potatoes, peeled, quartered, and cut into 1/2-inch pieces

- 1 loaf soda bread, optional
- 2 cloves garlic, finely chopped
- 1 teaspoon salt, plus more to taste
- 1/2 cup vegetable oil, or as needed
- 2 large yellow onions, thinly sliced
- 1/2 pound thick-sliced bacon, diced

Directions

1. In a large frying pan, sauté the bacon. Drain the fat and reserve both the bacon and the fat.

2. In a large mixing bowl, place the lamb, salt, pepper, and flour. Toss to coat the meat evenly.

3. Without cleaning, reheat the frying pan you used to fry the bacon. In batches, brown the lamb in the reserved bacon fat. If you run out of fat, use some of the vegetable oil.

4. Transfer the browned meat to a 10-quart stovetop casserole, leaving about 1/4 cup of fat in the frying pan.

5. Add the garlic and the chopped yellow onion to the pan and sauté until the onion begins to color a bit

6. Add the garlic-onion mixture to the casserole, along with the reserved bacon pieces, beef stock, and sugar.

7. Cover and simmer for 1 1/2 hours, or until the lamb is tender.

8. Add the carrots, the sliced onions, potatoes, thyme, bay leaf, and wine to the pot and simmer, covered, for about 20 minutes, or until the vegetables are tender. Taste test and add salt and pepper as needed.

9. Top with the parsley garnish before serving and accompany with soda bread.

35-Sausage (bangers) & Mash

PREPPING TIME: 25 MIN   SERVES: 2   **COOKING TIME:** 30 MIN

Ingredients

- ¼ cup butter
- 2 cups red wine
- 6 cups beef broth
- 1 tablespoon butter
- 4 links pork sausage
- 2 large onions, chopped
- 2 tablespoons milk (Optional)
- 1 teaspoon dry mustard powder
- 2 pounds potatoes, peeled and cubed
- salt and ground black pepper to taste

Directions

1. Preheat the oven to 200 degrees F (95 degrees C).

2. Cook the sausage links in a skillet over medium-low heat until browned on all sides, about 5 minutes per side; transfer to an oven-safe dish and move to the preheated oven to keep warm.

3. Place potatoes into a saucepan over medium heat, cover with water, and boil gently until potatoes are tender, 10 to 15 minutes. Drain and allow to steam dry for a minute or two. Mix in 1/4 cup of butter, milk, dry mustard, salt, and black pepper; mash until fluffy and smooth. Set aside.

4. Melt 1 tablespoon butter in a skillet over medium-high heat; cook the onions until translucent and just starting to brown, about 8 minutes. Pour in the beef broth and red wine; boil the mixture down to about half its volume, about 10 minutes. Season with salt and black pepper. To serve, place a sausage onto a serving plate with about 1/2 cup of mashed potatoes. Pour the onion gravy over the sausage and potatoes.

36-Livers & Onions

PREPPING TIME: 20 MIN   **SERVES:** 2   **COOKING TIME:** 25 MIN

Ingredients

- ¼ cup butter, divided+ dry mustard
- salt and pepper to taste
- 2 pounds sliced beef liver
- 1 ½ cups milk, or as needed
- 2 cups all-purpose flour, or as needed
- 2 large Vidalia(yellow) onions, sliced into rings
- chives/curly parsley to garnish
- 2 lbs potatoes for Mash +1/4 cup butter milk

Directions

1. Rinse the liver and pat dry. Cut into strips of 1.2 cm 1/4inches. Place in a small bowl filled with the cold milk. Soak for 30minutes to an hour. This will remove some of the metallic taste that the liver may have from its iron content.

2. While the livers are soaking start making the mashed potatoes If you wish to serve it with potatoes.

3. Place potatoes into a saucepan over medium heat, cover with water, and boil gently until potatoes are tender, 10 to 15 minutes. Drain and allow to steam dry for a minute or two. Mix in 1/4 cup of butter, milk, dry mustard, salt, and black pepper; mash until fluffy and smooth. Set aside.

4. Melt 2 tablespoons of butter in a skillet over medium-high heat; cook the onions until translucent and soft. Remove onion rings and melt the remaining butter.

5. Season the flour with salt& pepper and place in a shallow dish.

6. Drain the milk from the liver and coat the livers in the flour mixture.

47

36-Livers & Onions

PREPPING TIME: 20 MIN   **SERVES:** 2   **COOKING TIME:** 25 MIN

Directions

7. When the butter has melted, turn heat to medium-high and place coated livers in the pan. Fry livers till they're brown on the bottom 5-8 min and turn and cook on the other side until browned.

8. Add onions and reduce heat to medium. Cook for another 5-10 min. You can cook the liver to your preference.

Serve with mashed potato or any starch of your choice! Enjoy!

37-Piri Piri/Peri-Peri Flame grilled Chicken

PREPPING TIME: 30 MIN-1HR   **SERVES:** 2   **COOKING TIME:** 30 MIN

Ingredients

FOR THE Piri Piri/Peri-Peri CHICKEN

- 6 chicken legs, wings, or breast (You decide)
- 1 tablespoon smoked paprika
- 1 tablespoon garlic powder
- 1 tsp Salt and pepper to taste

FOR THE PERI-PERI MARINADE INGREDIENTS(marinate the chicken overnight for best results!)

- 1 pound red chilies chopped – African Bird's Eye peppers are traditional, but you can sub with habanero/serrano or Thai Chilli peppers
- 4 cloves garlic chopped
- 1 teaspoon smoked paprika you can sub in other chili powders
- 1/2 cup chopped cilantro
- 1/4 cup chopped basil
- 1/2 cup olive oil or vegetable oil
- Juice from 1 lemon
- Salt to taste (and black pepper, if desired)
- **FOR SERVING:** Chopped parsley, spicy chili flakes

37-Piri Piri/Peri-Peri Flame grilled Chicken

PREPPING TIME: 30 MIN-1HR   **SERVES:** 2   **COOKING TIME:** 30 MIN

Directions

1. Pat Chicken legs or wings or whichever pieces you choose dry and rub them down with paprika, garlic and salt, and black pepper. Cover & set aside.

2. If you are going to use your broiler or oven to grill, turn it on to 400F While preparing chicken.

I prefer charcoal/Wood fired Flame-grilled chicken

3. For the peri-peri sauce, add the Chili peppers, garlic, paprika, cilantro, and basil to a food processor. Process until well mixed.

4. Drizzle in the olive oil while continuing to process until the mixture thickens up.

5. Stir in lemon juice and adjust for salt.

6. Pour half of the Peri-Peri sauce over the chicken and mix the chicken to ensure it's fully coated. Cover the bowl and refrigerate for 30 min to an hour. (For best results marinate overnight)

7. Bake/Broil the chicken for 35-40 minutes, or until the chicken is cooked through. They should measure 165 degrees F internally, when measured with a meat thermometer or Flame grill over a charcoal fire for 30-40 min constantly turning every 5 min to prevent burning (My favorite and the authentic way to make this dish)

8. Once the chicken is cooked toss it into the remaining half of the Peri-Peri sauce. Garnish with chopped parsley and chili flakes. *Enjoy!*

Serve with fries, mashed potatoes or a salad!

38-Crispy chicken schnitzels with creamy mushroom sauce

Ingredients

Chicken Schnitzels

- Chicken schnitzels
- 4 large chicken breasts approx 100g or 4 ounces each
- 4 tablespoons / 30 grams cornflour/cornstarch
- 2 large eggs
- 1 tablespoon dijon mustard
- 1 cup panko breadcrumbs add extra if needed
- 2 – 3 tablespoons olive oil for frying the schnitzels

Mushroom Sauce

- 1 large onion finely diced
- 5 ounces / 150 grams sliced white mushrooms
- 2 ounces / 60 grams butter for frying the mushrooms
- 1.5 tablespoon / 15 grams cornflour/cornstarch
- 1½ cups / 360ml milk
- ½ cup / 120 ml single cream
- Salt to taste
- Ground black pepper to taste

38-Crispy chicken schnitzels with creamy mushroom sauce

PREPPING TIME: 30 MIN-1HR   **SERVES:** 2   **COOKING TIME:** 25 MIN

Directions

Chicken Schnitzels

1. Butterfly the chicken breasts by cutting them almost in half, then open them out and press flat. Sprinkle with salt to taste.

2. 4 large chicken breasts,salt

3. Place the cornflour in one flat dish.

4. 4 tablespoons / 30 grams cornflour/cornstarch

5. Break the eggs into the second dish and whisk in 1 tablespoon dijon mustard.

6. 2 large eggs,1 tablespoon dijon mustard

7. Place 1 cup of breadcrumbs into the third dish. (See note 1).

8. 1 cup panko breadcrumbs

9. Coat each schnitzel by dipping first into the cornflour, then into the beaten egg, and finally into the breadcrumbs. Press the breadcrumbs firmly onto the chicken.

10. Place the schnitzels on a plate and put them into the refrigerator to rest for half an hour. This will allow the coating to firm up and help to prevent it from falling off while frying.

11. Fry the schnitzels in 2 tablespoons of olive oil for 5 minutes per side until golden brown and crispy. See note 2.

12. 2 – 3 tablespoons olive oil

38-Crispy chicken schnitzels with creamy mushroom sauce

PREPPING TIME: 30 MIN-1HR   **SERVES:** 2   **COOKING TIME:** 25 MIN

Directions

Creamy Mushroom Sauce

1. Sauté the chopped onions and mushrooms in the butter in a saucepan until the onions are softened and the mushrooms have released their moisture (about 5 minutes).

2. 1 large onion, 150 grams sliced white mushrooms,2 ounces / 60 grams butter

3. Once the onions have softened, remove from the heat and stir in 1½ tablespoons corn flour/cornstarch.

4. 1.5 tablespoon / 15 grams corn flour/cornstarch

5. Add the milk and single cream.

6. 1½ cups / 360ml milk,½ cup / 120 ml single cream

7. Return to the heat and bring to the boil, stirring continuously until the mixture thickens. Reduce the heat to low and allow to simmer for 2 minutes. See note 4.

8. Season with salt and ground black pepper to taste.

9. salt, ground black pepper

10. *Serve the chicken schnitzels on a plate with mashed potatoes, vegetables, salad or baked fries. Your choice! Spoon over the sauce and enjoy.*

39-Pastitsio(Greek Lasagne)

PREPPING TIME: 40 MIN   SERVES: 2   COOKING TIME: 1 HR 25 MIN

Ingredients

Main Dish

- 2 medium red onions chopped
- 4 tablespoons unsalted butter
- 2 lbs 90% lean ground beef
- ⅛ tsp ground cumin
- 1 ½ teaspoon Salt & 1 1/2 tsp pepper to taste (based on our preference)
- ½ cup water
- 2 tablespoons tomato paste
- 3 large eggs, beaten
- 2.5 cups Bucatini or Ziti Pasta
- 1 cup crumbled feta cheese
- 1cup cooking red wine
- ½ tsp cinnamon powder
- ¼ tsp ground cloves
- 3 cloves garlic
- 1 small bay leaf
- 2 beef bouillon cubes

Bechamel Sauce

- 6 tablespoons unsalted butter
- ¾ cup all-purpose flour
- 4 cups whole milk warmed
- 1 ½ tsp salt
- 3 large eggs
- 1 teaspoon ground nutmeg
- 12-16oz Ounces Kasseri/kefalotyri(Sheep's milk Greek Cheese) grated Parmesan can be substituted for Romano Cheese)

39-Pastitsio(Greek Lasagne)

PREPPING TIME: 30 MIN-1HR   **SERVES: 2**   **COOKING TIME:** 1 HR 25MIN

Directions

Meat Sauce

1. Heat in a large pot over high heat. Add garlic and onion, cook for 2 – 3 minutes until onion is softened. Add beef and cook, breaking it up as you go, until it changes from red to brown.

2. Add wine and cook until the wine has mostly evaporated – about 3 minutes.

3. Add remaining Meat Sauce ingredients. Stir well, bring to simmer, then reduce heat to medium / medium low so it's simmering gently. Cook for 45 min to 1 hour until liquid is mostly gone, stirring every now and then. It should be a thick mixture with little liquid, not saucy like Spaghetti Bolognese.

4. Remove from the stove and cool. Preferably to room temperature, otherwise for at least 30 minutes before assembling (lid off).

GREEK BÉCHAMEL

1. Melt butter in a large saucepan over medium heat. Add flour and stir for 1 minute.

2. While stirring, slowly pour half the milk in. It should turn into a wet paste. Then again, while stirring, pour in remaining milk – the paste should easily dissolve so it's lump-free. If not, just whisk vigorously.

3. Cook, stirring so the base doesn't catch, for 5 minutes or until thick enough so it coats the back of a wooden spoon thickly and you can draw a path across it with your finger.

4. Remove from the stove. Stir in nutmeg, cheese and salt.

5. Leave to cool for 5 minutes. Then whisk in egg yolks quickly. Place the lid on and set aside. If sauce cools and gets too thick to pour, just reheat on a low stove until pourable.

39-Pastitsio(Greek Lasagne)

PREPPING TIME: 30 MIN-1HR   **SERVES:** 2   **COOKING TIME:** 1 HR 25MIN

Directions

Pasta

1. When you're ready to assemble, cook the pasta per packet instructions, minus 1 minute.
2. Drain, then return to the pot. Leave to cool for 3 minutes, then stir through egg whites. Gently stir through crumbled feta.

ASSEMBLE AND BAKE:

1. Preheat the oven to 180°C/350°F (all oven types).
2. Place pasta in a DEEP baking dish (33 x 22 x 7 cm / 9 x 13 x 2.75"), arranging them so they are all going in the same direction as best you can (for visual effect when sliced). Make the surface as level as you can.
3. Top with Meat Sauce, then smooth the surface.
4. Pour over Béchamel Sauce, then sprinkle over the cheese.
5. Bake for 30 min or until the crust turns golden.
6. Cool for at least 10-25 minutes so you can cut into neat pieces and you may reheat after, if needed.

40-PERI PERI/Piri Piri Prawns/Tiger Shrimp

PREPPING TIME: 1HR& 25 MIN   **SERVES:** 2   **COOKING TIME:** 25 MIN

Ingredients

- Jumbo prawns/Tiger Shrimp – one kilogram (deveined, heads on/off) thawed
- 1/2 cup melted garlic butter& Olive oil to fry
- Lemon juice – two tablespoons
- Paprika – 2 tablespoons
- Fresh Thai/African bird eye chili - 6 finely blended
- dried Chili flakes – 1 teaspoon
- Garlic – 2 cloves roasted (Wrap in foil and place in oven)
- Salt – teaspoon
- Chopped flat leaf parsley to Garnish

Directions

1. Place shrimp in a bowl and add garlic butter
2. Add the roasted garlic.
3. Add the chilies and paprika.
5. Add the lemon juice and salt.
7. Add the prawns and allow to marinate for at least an hour in the refrigerator (the longer, the better)
8. Heat a griddle pan with olive oil. (You can charcoal BBQ too)
9. Grill/Fry the prawns/Shrimp until cooked(Turns light pink) Don't overcook shrimp they cook Fast
10. Transfer them to serving small plates. Sprinkle with chili flakes & Garnish with Parsley

Serve with Portuguese rice or freshly fried chips/fries or a salad

41-Prego No Pao (Steak Roll)

PREPPING TIME: 15 MIN   SERVES: 2   COOKING TIME: 25 MIN

Ingredients

- 2 white fresh bread rolls
- 2 beef steaks
- 2 garlic cloves
- 1 bay leaf
- 1 tbsp butter
- 1 tsp olive oil
- Salt and black pepper
- Yellow mustard
- 2 tablespoon white wine
- 1 Sprig thyme
- ½ cup red wine
- ⅓ tomato puree
- 2 tablespoons peri peri sauce

Directions

1. Gently pound the steak to tenderize it (if you don't have a tenderizer, a rolling pin works well).

2. Roughly chop the garlic, then place it on top of the meat. Gently pound it again, crushing the garlic into the meat. Season it with salt and black pepper.

3. Place a medium frying pan over high heat Or for the best results flame grill over a Charcoal/wood fire and char on both sides.

4. If you are frying: Once hot, add the butter, olive oil and a bay leaf.

5. If you are bbqing remove when charred and place in frying pan with butter, bay leaf and olive oil

6. If using a thin steak, you should need less than 2 minutes on each side.

7. Remove the steak from the frying pan, reduce the heat to low, add tomato puree, thyme and peri peri sauce and add white wine. Stir till a sauce has thickened.

8. Add steaks back into pan and allow to marinate in sauce for a few minutes

9. Cut the bread in half and quickly toast it on another pan/griddle. Spread a good amount of mustard & the sauce over the bread, place your steak on top.

Serve warm, with a salad or any favorite side and an Ice cold drink and enjoy!

42-Boerewors sausage(South-African Sausage)

PREPPING TIME: 1HR& 45 MIN   **SERVES:** 3   **COOKING TIME:** 25 MIN

Ingredients

- 2 lb beef roast, (top round roast or brisket), trimmed off excess tissue
- 1 lb fatty pork shoulder/butt, or pork neck or belly
- 1 Tablespoon ground coriander seeds
- 1 Tablespoon salt
- ½ teaspoon ground allspice
- ½ teaspoon ground black pepper
- ¼ teaspoon ground nutmeg
- 1/8 teaspoon ground cloves
- ¼ cup malt vinegar
- hog casing for fresh sausage(Can be purchased online)

Directions

Preparing the Meat

1. Cube the beef and pork into pieces that will fit easily into your meat grinder. Sprinkle the spices over meat and mix to coat. Cover the seasoned meat and refrigerate for at least 1 hour.

2. After the meat has rested, follow the instructions that came with your meat grinder to grind the seasoned meat using the coarse grinding blade.*

3. Add the vinegar to the ground meat and mix well.

Stuffing the Sausage

1. Thoroughly rinse (inside and out) one salted hog casing. Prepare the casing for stuffing as directed on the casing package.

2. If using a Kitchen Aid, or similar, mixer, attach the thick sausage stuffer attachment to the meat grinder attachment.

42-Boerewors sausage(South African Sausage)

PREPPING TIME: 1HR 45MIN   **SERVES:** 3   **COOKING TIME:** 25 MIN

Directions

3. Place the entire casing onto the sausage stuffer attachment, leaving 4 inches hanging off the end. Tie a knot in this end of the casing to keep your sausage mixture from oozing out. Begin to stuff your casing as directed for your machine, moving slowly and being careful not to over-stuff the casing. (Don't worry too much about unevenly stuffed sausage, we will take care of that later.)

4. As you stuff the casing, coil the sausage onto a large plate. Stop stuffing when you only have 5-6 inches of casing left. Remove the casing from the sausage stuffer attachment.

5. Before you knot the end, check the sausage for uneven areas. If you find any, gently even out the sausage mixture in the casing with your hands.

6. Once the sausage is even to your liking, knot the end of the casing.

7. If you still have additional sausage mixture (for us, this recipe made two 1.5 lb sausages), rinse and prepare another casing and stuff it as before.

8. Once all your sausage mixture has been stuffed, refrigerate your sausages overnight (at least 12 hours) so that the flavors can come together before cooking.

42-Boerewors sausage(South African Sausage)

PREPPING TIME: 1HR 45MIN   **SERVES:** 3   **COOKING TIME:** 25MIN

Directions

Cooking the Sausage

1. The traditional way to cook boerewors is on the Charcoal grill. Heat your grill to a medium-high heat (400F). (You should be able to hold your hand a few inches from the cooking grate for 4-5 seconds.) If desired, soak a large wooden skewer or two in water.Place the boerewors onto the grill and cook for 4-5 minutes on the first side, until the color has changed and the sausage has nice grill marks. Flip the boerewors and cook for 3-4 minutes on the second side, until the sausage is firm. Cook till your preferred meat preference.

2. Remove the sausage from the grill and place on a large platter to serve.

Boerewors can be purchased online too or you can ask your butcher to grind your meat for you and you just add the seasonings and do the stuffings on your own.

43-South African Pepper steak pie 🇬🇧

PREPPING TIME: MIN   **SERVES: 2**   **COOKING TIME:** MIN

Ingredients

- 2 lbs beef chuck steak, cubed (Short-rib could work too!)
- 1 large onion, sliced
- 3 tablespoon brandy
- 3 teaspoon beef stock powder
- 3 teaspoon freshly ground black pepper
- 1 teaspoon chopped thyme (optional)
- 1 1/2 cups lager
- 1 cup water
- Thawed puff pastry
- 2 tablespoon flour
- 1/2 teaspoon salt
- 2 tablespoon olive oil, for frying

Directions

1. Preheat oven to 350F. Toss meat in seasoned flour and brown with onion in hot oil. Deglaze your pan with brandy. Add the beer, water, stock powder, pepper, and thyme. Cover and bake for 45 minutes or until meat is tender.

2. Remove from the oven and cool slightly. Increase the oven to 400F. Lay 2 pastry sheets flat and cut evenly sized rectangles. I got 6 large rectangles per sheet, and there are 2 sheets in a package. 24 rectangles = 6 pies.(You can make smaller pies if preferred) .Cover a large baking sheet with baking paper and place 12 rectangles on it. Add a good amount of filling to each and cover with the remaining puff pastry. I didn't roll the pastry out, but you might have to stretch the ones that'll go on top a bit to accommodate the filling. Use a fork to crimp the edges.

3. Beat an egg and brush on top of pies. Bake for 20-25 minutes. Serve immediately!

44-The Gatsby Sandwich

PREPPING TIME: 30 MIN   SERVES: 2   COOKING TIME: 25 MIN

Ingredients

- 1 tbsp. canola oil
- 6 slices bologna
- 1/3 cup ketchup
- cheese slices
- Piri-piri sauce, to taste
- 1 (8″) crusty Italian roll, toasted
- 1/2 cup shredded iceberg lettuce
- 2 cups Home fried thick-cut french fries, try not iver fry or make too crispy. (The key to soft fries known as Slap Tjips in South africa) is rinse the potatoes after slicing them and soak them in cold water for 20 min. Remove and half cook them in oil. When they are partially soft remove from the heat and wait 5min and then resubmerge in the hot oil.

Directions

1. Heat oil in a 10″ skillet over medium-high heat and add bologna; cook, turning once, until browned, 1–2 minutes. Split roll and top bottom half with bologna. Cover with fries, ketchup, and piri-piri. Add lettuce; cover with top half of roll.

45-Trifle Tart: Mixed Fruit,Cake And Custard

PREPPING TIME: 25 MIN **SERVES: 2** **FRIDGE TIME: 1HR**

Ingredients

ingredients for English Trifle

For the custard layer you can use English Powdered custard or purchase ready made custard)

(If you decide to use Bird's Custard powder, make two batches (2 pints) following the instructions on the back of the can.)

- 4 cups whole milk
- 8 egg yolks (warmed up)
- 1/2 cup sugar
- 4 tablespoon cornstarch
- 1 1/2 teaspoon vanilla extract
- 1/2 cup butter

- P.S: You can use canned custard too. This is what I do.

Whipped cream

- 1 1/2 cups heavy whipping cream
- 1 teaspoon powdered sugar

For the cake layer

- 9×13 white or yellow cake/Pound cake
- 1/2 cup sherry wine(sweetened type)
- 3 heaping tablespoons seedless red raspberry jam or preserves

For the fruit layer

- 2 cups sliced fresh strawberries
- 1 cup fresh raspberries
- 1 cup canned peaches
- 1 tablespoon sherry wine, preferably the sweetened type
- 1 tablespoon sugar
- 1 box jelly/jello PEPARE THE DAY BEFORE(Optional)

(Pick however many fruit you may want)

64

45-Trifle Tart: Mixed Fruit, Cake And Custard

PREPPING TIME: 25 MIN   SERVES: 2   FRIDGE TIME: 1HR

Directions

1. To make the custard begin by heating the milk in a saucepan. You just want it to come to a simmer, you'll see steam rising from the surface as well. (If you are using Bird's custard, follow the preparation instructions on the canister for two pints.)

2. In a bowl, whisk the egg yolks together with the sugar and cornstarch.

3. and pour everything back into the saucepan with low heat to thicken. You need to do it slowly so you don't burn it, but custard can be finicky, so you need to make sure it heats enough to bubble for several minutes.

Use a sturdy rubber spatula to stir the liquid and keep it from sticking to the bottom of the pan. Remove from heat and whisk in vanilla.

Let sit for 5 minutes, then whisk in butter. Custard will be thick and smooth.

4. Let custard cool down

5. Because you are brushing the cake with sherry, you want the cake pieces to be small enough to soak it up.

6. Place all those pieces cut-side up and brush them with the sherry. Now spread the jam/preserves on top. Cut them into small squares.

7. chop fresh strawberries and use fresh raspberries as well. When you're ready to assemble the trifle, layer one-third of the cake cubes, jam/preserve side up, in the bottom of the trifle dish.

8. Cover with one-third of the fruit and jelly/jello (If you choose to add this).

9. Add one-third of the custard.

10. Finally, top with one-third of the whipped cream.

11. Now repeat those layers two more times. Garnish with fresh sliced strawberries or raspberries and chill in the refrigerator until ready to serve.

46-Melktert: A south African Dutch Style Milk tart

PREPPING TIME: 30 MIN   **SERVES:** 2   **COOKING TIME:** 40 MIN

Ingredients

(Pastry Crust)
- 1 1/2 cups (355ml) all-purpose flour
- 1/3 cup (35grams) confectioner's sugar powdered sugar
- ¼ teaspoon salt
- 9 Tablespoons (137ml) unsalted butter (cold or frozen) , cut into small pieces
- 1 large egg yolk.

Milk filling
- 2 1/4 (496 ml) cups milk
- 2 tablespoon (30ml) butter
- 2 tablespoons (37 ml) flour
- 3-4 tablespoons (25-27ml) cornstarch
- 1/2 cup (100grams) Granulated sugar
- 2 Large eggs
- 2 teaspoons vanilla extract
- ½ teaspoon almond extract (optional)
- ½ teaspoon cinnamon
- ½ teaspoon nutmeg or replace with cinnamon

46-Melktert: A south African Dutch Style Milk tart

PREPPING TIME: MIN   **SERVES: 2**   **COOKING TIME: 40** MIN

Directions

1. Butter or spray a 9-inch pie pan with a removable bottom – making sure it is has been adequately sprayed. Set aside

2. Place flour, salt and sugar in a food processor pulse for a couple of times to
mix ingredients.

3. Throw in butter and pulse until rough dough forms.

4. Then add egg yolk - pulse until the dough barely comes together.

5. Remove dough place on a work surface - knead just enough to incorporate all the dough. Working the dough as little as possible.

6. **Do not overwork the dough**; otherwise it'll be too tough. When it's ready, the dough will be barely moistened and come together into a ball.

7. Lightly press the dough on the prepare pie pan – working from the center up until the bottom and sides are fully covered with pastry – again be very gentle when pressing the dough onto the pie pan.

46-Melktert: A south African Dutch Style Milk tart

PREPPING TIME: 35MIN	SERVES: 2	COOKING TIME: 40MIN

Directions

8. Place pie pan in the freezer and freeze for at least 30 minutes or more this helps prevent the dough from rising- if you are in a rush brick, then bake with beans to prevent rising.

9. Preheat oven to 400 degrees F (205 degrees C) and place rack in center of oven.

10. Bake crust for about 20 to 25 minutes or until the crust is dry and golden browned. Set aside.

You can use premade crusts with GRAHAM CRACKERS TOO

Milk Filling

1. Place saucepan over medium heat, add butter, nutmeg and milk -bring to a boil and remove from the heat.

2. In another bowl, mix together flour, cornstarch, sugar, vanilla and almond extract- whisk in eggs until smooth. Gently whisk into the saucepan making sure there are no lumps

3. Now return the pan back on the stove – keep stirring constantly until in starts to bubble.

4. Cook for about 5-6 minutes. Remove from heat and pour mixture into the baked pastry shell Sprinkle with cinnamon. Chill until ready to be served.

47-Peppermint Fridge tart

PREPPING TIME: 30 MIN   **SERVES: 2**   **FRIDGE TIME:**   OVERNIGHT

Ingredients

(Refrigeration: overnight)

- 1 can caramel condensed milk + 500ml cream
- 35gm peppermint crisp chocolate (you'll find this in the international section or a South African shop) or Aero bubbly mint or Cadbury chocolate with mint
- 1 packet of thin coconut biscuits (Tennis biscuits are best - find in the international section or a South
- African shop) / or Arnott's Nice biscuits, or any coconut biscuit (preferably square shaped)

Directions

1. Whip cream till thick. Add caramel and mix well till combined.

2. Place a layer of biscuits in a suitable dish (preferably square or rectangular) - don't worry if there are small spaces in-between.

3.Spoon a little bit of the caramel mixture over the biscuits to cover completely cover

Grate a piece of the chocolate over caramel mixture.

4.Repeat with layering biscuits, caramel and grated chocolate until finished, ending with a caramel & chocolate layer.

5.Shred chocolate with peppermint at the top

6.Place in fridge to set for a few hours or overnight if you can.

48-South African Indian Gulab Jamin

PREPPING TIME: 40 MIN   **SERVES: 2**   **COOKING TIME:** 35 MIN

Ingredients

- 150 ml condensed milk
- 2 Tablespoon unsalted butter melted
- 1/4 cup milk
- 1/4 teaspoon nutmeg (ground)
- 1/4 cup powdered milk (optional)
- 1&1/4 cup self-raising flour
- vegetable oil for frying
- 1/2 teaspoon cardamom/elachie (ground)
- 1/2 cup desiccated coconut for dusting after dipping in syrup
- Parchment paper

Syrup

- 2 cups water
- 1 & 1/2 cup granulated sugar
- 1/4 teaspoon rose essence
- 1/2 teaspoon cardamom/elachie

48-South African Indian Gulab Jamun

PREPPING TIME: 40 MIN   SERVES: 2   COOKING TIME: 35 MIN

Directions

1. For the syrup, add the sugar, water, Cardamom and rose essence to a saucepan and simmer on medium to low heat until it's slightly sticky and syrupy. Takes about 20-25 minutes to thicken. Reduce heat to the lowest setting and keep syrup warm.

2. In a large dish, add the condensed milk, melted ghee/unsalted butter, milk, nutmeg and Cardamom. Mix it well. Add the powdered milk and a little flour at a time until you form a soft dough, not too sticky and not too dry, you must be able to roll it into shape easily. You may require more or less flour. If the dough feels too sticky when bringing it together, wash your hands and knead again. It will feel less sticky. You can also rub a little ghee on your hands when rolling the dough into shape

3. Heat oil on medium heat in a small saucepan. Divide dough into little balls and then roll in the palm of your hands to form an oval finger shape. Keep checking the temperature of your oil, if it gets too hot reduce the temperature or turn the heat off completely to allow it to cool down a little.

4. Fry the Gulab Jamuns in the oil, use a slotted spoon to drain all the oil before removing. Dip in the warmed syrup for a few seconds and roll into the coconut 5. Place on parchment paper until it cools down and then store in an airtight container.

49-Maalvapoeding/malva pudding
Dutch style sponge cake

PREPPING TIME: 35 MIN   SERVES: 2   COOKING TIME: 45 MIN

Ingredients

For the batter

- 1 tablespoon butter (at room temperature)
- 1 cup sugar
- 2 eggs
- 1 tablespoon apricot jam
- 1 teaspoon baking soda
- ½ cup milk
- ¼ cup brown vinegar (e.g. malt or balsamic vinegar)
- 1 cup flour , sifted
- ¼ teaspoon salt

For the sauce

- 1 cup heavy cream
- ¾ cup sugar
- 8 tablespoons butter
- ½ cup hot water
- 1 teaspoon vanilla essence

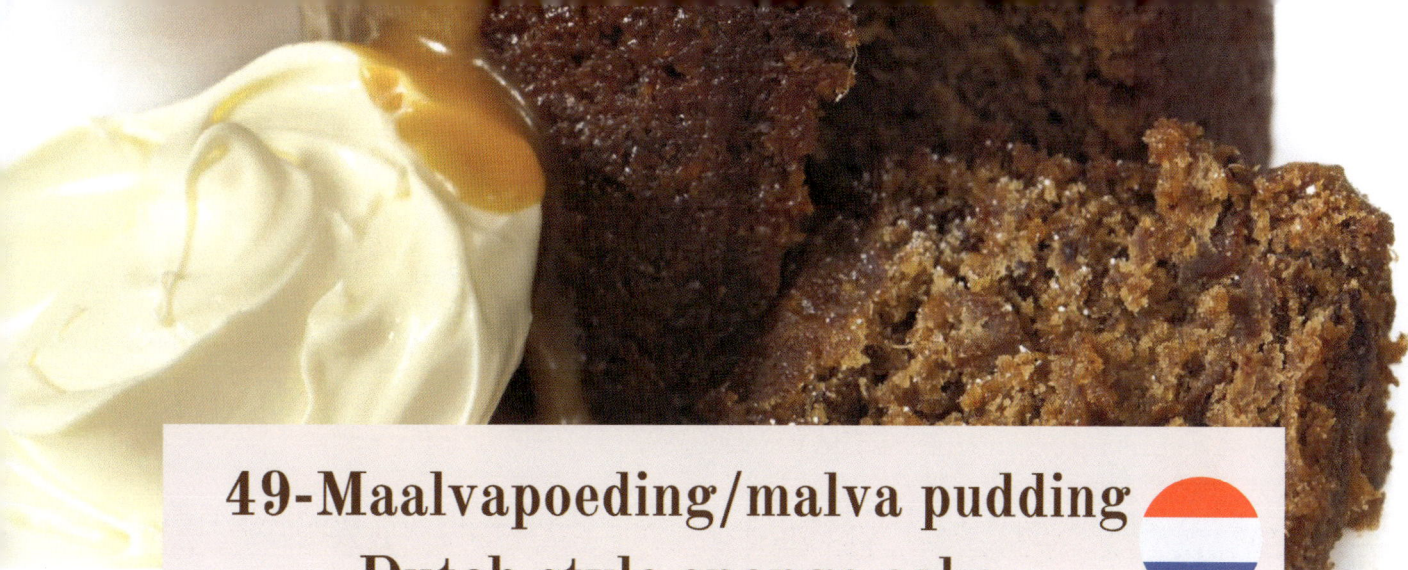

49-Maalvapoeding/malva pudding
Dutch style sponge cake

PREPPING TIME: 35 MIN   **SERVES:** 2   **COOKING TIME:** 45 MIN

Directions

1. Preheat oven to 350 F / 180 C.

2. Whip butter with sugar for 2 minutes. Then, add the eggs one at a time, and
continue to whip well after each addition.

3. Add the apricot jam and mix well.

4. Then, add the milk and the baking soda, then the brown vinegar.

5. Add the sifted flour gradually and continue to mix.

6. Pour batter into a 9-inch (22 cm) square greased baking pan.

7. Bake for 45 minutes in the oven or until an inserted toothpick comes out clean.

8. While the malva pudding is baking, mix all the sauce ingredients in a saucepan on medium/high heat.

9. Bring to a boil, then remove from heat. Cover.

10. Remove the pudding from the oven, then pour the sauce on top. Set aside for 15 minutes before serving so that the cake has time to absorb the sauce to
saturation.

11. Serve with warm custard, vanilla ice cream or whipped cream.

50-Koesister (Cape Malay Doughnuts)

PREPPING TIME: 60 MIN   **SERVES: 2**   **COOKING TIME:** 30 MIN

Ingredients

- 1 100g potato
- 300 g cake flour
- 4 tablespoons of granulated sugar
- a pinch Sea salt
- 1 teaspoon ground ginger
- 1 teaspoon ground cinnamon
- 1 teaspoon ground aniseed
- 1/4 teaspoon ground cardamom
- 1 teaspoon dried ground clementine peel
- 1 teaspoon fresh clementine zest
- 3 1/2 cups sunflower oil
- 1/2 cup warm milk
- 1/2 cup warm water
- 2 tsp dry active yeast
- 1 free range egg, lightly beaten

For the syrup

- 300 g granulated sugar
- 1 cup water

For the coconut coating

- 500 g desiccated coconut
- 1 teaspoon dried clementine peel
- 1 tsp ground cinnamon
- 1/2 teaspoon fresh Clementine zest

50-Koesister (Cape Malay Doughnuts)

PREPPING TIME: 60 MIN   **SERVES:** 2   **COOKING TIME:** 30 MIN

Directions

1. Boil the potato in its skin. Then, while still hot, peel and mash until smooth.

2. Sift the flour, 4 tablespoons of the sugar, and salt. Stir in the spices and Clementine peel.

3. Rub in 4 Tablespoon of oil and the potato to form a crumbly mixture.

4. Mix the milk and water, then add the yeast and 1 tsp sugar, then mix to dissolve.

5. Add the milk mixture and egg to the dry ingredients and mix well to form a very soft and sticky dough.

6. Moisten your hands with a little oil and rub them over the dough, cover, and set aside for two hours, or until doubled in size.

7. Generously coat your hands in oil and knead down the dough.

8. Place on a well-oiled surface and divide into 12-16 balls. Again, allow the dough to double in size (30-40 minutes)

9. Heat the remaining oil in a large saucepan and, when hot, fry the koesisters until golden. Drain on kitchen paper.

10. Place the koesisters in the syrup and place them over low heat to soak for at least 20 minutes.

11. Remove from the syrup and roll in the coconut mixture. Serve warm.

To make the syrup, dissolve the sugar in the water over low heat. Once dissolved, bring the syrup to a boil and cook for 5 minutes.

To make the coconut coating, place the coconut, dried clementine peel, and cinnamon in a pan and toast until golden brown. Allow to cool, then add the fresh clementine zest.

Cooking; like traveling, is an experience of exploring diverse food flavors and profiles. Tasting the regional cuisines and learning how to prepare them; connects us to the land where each recipe transpired from. With a Rich History of heritage and spice influences, along with its 11 official languages and culinary Options; I hope that you walk away learning a little more about how diverse South Africa is. Food always tells a story about people and places.

About the Author

I'm a 5th generation South African whose great, great, grandparents came from the Southern region(Puducherry) Tamil Nadu; on the Southeast coast of India. They embarked on the indentured labor migration journey with nothing but the clothes on their back and hope for a better life. My family experienced the hardship of working on the sugarcane plantations and then the divisive legislation and economic dysfunctions of apartheid. Laboring was all they ever knew and continued farming. They managed to climb out of poverty when apartheid ended. I created this book with a grateful heart, knowing that now that I reside in the USA, I have the ability to create the things that I care about and share them with the world. As I selected a portion of some of the recipes, that were foods I grew up eating, I definitely took a trip down memory lane. I thought about the history of food, spices, and people. About how food changed as it was taken to other regions. I also thought about how locals added their own twist to the dishes based on the availability of spices and agricultural produce and how resourceful people were. This creative spirit mixed with the survival and perseverance of people has led to new inventions of curries, stews, and flavorful dishes that became an iconic trademark distinct to that region. Whilst many dishes have influences from countries abroad, the recipes are now distinct to no other place than South Africa! Grab a plate and savor the flavor. Warm wishes and to many more tastebud adventures!

Stay Tuned for My next
creation:
Modern daily cuisines with
African inspired flavors
and fusions.